KV-489-352

European Issues in Children's
Identity and Citizenship **3**

# Political Learning and
# Citizenship in Europe

*Edited by Christine Roland-Lévy and Alistair Ross*

Children's
Identity &
Citizenship
in Europe

**Trentham Books**
Stoke on Trent, UK and Sterling USA

**Trentham Books Limited**

| | |
|---|---|
| Westview House | 22883 Quicksilver Drive |
| 734 London Road | Sterling |
| Oakhill | VA 20166-2012 |
| Stoke on Trent | USA |
| Staffordshire | |
| England ST4 5NP | |

2003 © Christine Roland-Lévy and Alistair Ross

First published 2003

**British Library Cataloguing-in-Publication Data**
A catalogue record for this book is available from the British Library

1 85856 276 7

Designed and typeset by Trentham Print Design Ltd., Chester and printed in Great Britain by Cromwell Press Ltd., Wiltshire.

# Contents

**Series introduction** • vii
*Alistair Ross*

Chapter Synopsis • ix

Chapter 1
**Introduction: Growing up politically in Europe today** • 1
*Alistair Ross and Christine Roland-Lévy*

Chapter 2
**Children's Political Learning: Concept-based approaches versus Issues-based approaches** • 17
*Alistair Ross*

Chapter 3
**Thinking and acting as citizens** • 34
Ian Davies and Tony Thorpe

Chapter 4
**Ethnocentric narratives and the 'European dimension' in historical education** • 53
Aristotle Kallis

Chapter 5
**Becoming political in different countries** • 78
Carole Hahn

Chapter 6
**Attitudes towards European Union citizenship** • 94
Dave Edye

Chapter 7
**The social and political learning needs of refugee students and asylum seekers from Third World Countries in Irish post-primary schools • 116**
*Maureen Killeavy*

Chapter 8
**Young people, citizenship and politics in Europe today • 126**
*Hélène Feertchak*

Chapter 9
**The introduction of the euro as a means to create a new feeling of territorial belonging • 147**
*Christine Roland-Lévy*

Chapter 10
**European values and political education • 161**
*Jan Kerkhofs*

**Notes on contributors • 177**

**Bibliography • 179**

**Index • 191**

# Series Introduction:
# European Issues in Children's
# Identity and Citizenship

*Political learning and citizenship in Europe* is the third volume in the series *European Issues in Children's Identity and Citizenship.* This series has arisen from the work of the ERASMUS Thematic Network Project called Children's Identity and Citizenship in Europe (CiCe). This network brings together over 90 University Departments, in 29 European states, all of whom share an interest in the education of professionals who will work with children and young people in the area of social, political and economic education. The Network links many of those who are educating the future teachers, youth workers, social pedagogues and social psychologists in Europe.

The CiCe Network began in 1996, and has been supported by the European Commission since 1998. It is now entering a major second phase of development, which will run to late 2005. This series arises from our conviction that changes in contemporary European society are such that we need to examine how the processes of socialisation are adapting to the new contexts. Political, economic and social changes are underway that suggest that we are developing multi-faceted and layered identities, that reflect the contingencies of European integration. In particular, children are growing up in this rapidly changing society, and their social behaviour will reflect the dimensions of this new and developing social unit. Identities will probably be rather different: national identities will continue alongside new identifications, with sub-national regions and supra-national unions. Our sense of citizenship will also develop in rather different ways than in the past: multiple and nested loyalties will develop, more complex than the simple affiliations of the past.

Those who will work with children and young people have a particular role to play in this. They will have to help young people develop their own relationships with the new institutions that develop, while at the same time being mindful of the traditional relationships known and understood by parents and grandparents, and their role in inter-generational acculturation.

This series is designed to discuss and debate the issues concerned with the professional and academic education of teachers, early childhood workers, social pedagogues and the like. They will need to understand the complex issues surrounding the socialisation and social understanding of the young, and to be aware of the similarities and differences in professional practices across Europe. They will need to work with young people learning to be citizens – citizens both of the traditional political entities, and of the developing new polities of Europe.

This volume, the third in the series, focuses particularly on the form and area of political learning. It is thematically linked to the preceding volume (on economic learning) and the volume that will follow, on social learning.

CiCe welcomes enquiries from potential members of the Network. These should be addressed to the CiCe Central Co-ordination Unit, at the Institute for Policy Studies in Education, London Metropolitan University, 166–220 Holloway Road, London N7 8DB, United Kingdom.

Alistair Ross
*Series Editor*

On behalf of the editorial committee: Tilman Alert, Marta Fulop, Akos Gocsal, Soren Hegstrup, Riitta Korhonen, Emilio Lastrucci, Elisabet Nasman, Panyota Papoulia-Tzelpi, Christine Roland-Lévy and Ann-Marie van Den Dries

# Chapter Synopsis

## Chapter One: Growing up politically in Europe today

This chapter introduces young people's political learning in contemporary Europe. 'Political learning' in this context means all the ways, formal and informal, by which these young members of society come to understand the rules, processes, institutions and patterns of behaviour that relate to the way in which societies organise themselves, allocate values and resources, and create and execute rules. Our focus is the period that is current for young people (which is rather shorter and more immediate than what is 'current' for older people), and we use 'Europe' in a loose cultural sense, not in a legalistic or formal sense. The central threads running through the various chapters in this book will amplify, explain and justify these definitions and qualifications. Our concerns are both with political socialisation and with political education. We suggest that an individual's identity can be seen as fluid and contingent, changing and responding to context and to personal and wider history, and that it is also initially and most powerfully formed in the early years of the individual's life. The identity – or identities – of a young adult are by no means immutable, but have already been formulated and expressed. Various aspects of identity develop between birth and adulthood: the sequence of construction is itself contingent on the social and political circumstances in which the individual grows up. Some of these aspects of identity are undoubtedly concerned with a political identity. This book is about a new and different political education: the result of change brought about partly by political, social and economic movements, and partly by an emerging new kind of 'territory' – not just a geographical territory but a territory of the shared collective mind. Europe is developing as a shared set of mental values that have the potential to develop as much a sense of shared identity as did the old nationalisms of the nineteenth century.

## Chapter Two: Children's Political Learning: Concept-based approaches versus Issues-based approaches

Political education with children is more talked about than practised. There is a relatively high level of rhetoric about education for citizenship, or for democracy, but there also appears to be a comparatively low level of practical activity. This chapter examines this, arguing that there is a divide between two approaches – concept-based approaches that offer an adult-determined agenda of structures and generalisation that is often hard to transmit, and issues-based approaches that are focused on children's interests, but which teachers find difficult to develop into more broadly based generalisations about political activity. If we are to get away from safe teaching about structures and processes, about the neutral and the bland, then we need to ensure that teachers are equipped with a wide conceptual understanding, with a knowledge of the issues that might illustrate these, and with the skills to manage covering the issues of participatory democracy through handling classroom political debate in ways that have not been supposed to have had a place in the classroom for a decade or more. Some preliminary investigation suggests that there is much work to be done in developing these skills.

## Chapter Three: Thinking and acting as citizens

This chapter discusses issues arising from a project in which classroom resources were produced for citizenship education. The Department for Education and Skills funded a project that focused on three procedural concepts of citizenship education i.e. explaining, tolerating and participating. A discussion about the nature of politics is followed by a consideration of procedural concepts, a description of the project structure and an evaluation of issues emerging from some of the initial work. We want, rather ambitiously, to help move the debate from questions such as 'should we have citizenship education?' to 'what should be seen as good work in citizenship education?' We describe the work of teachers in three curriculum areas (Personal and Social Education, History, English) and discuss how they have developed materials designed to help students become better at explaining, tolerating and participating. Finally, we draw attention to some issues that are guiding our existing evaluation of the project, indicating some of the challenges that lie ahead.

## Chapter Four: Ethnocentric narratives and the 'European dimension' in historical education

History is an essential constituent element of the construction of an individual's or a group's identity. It is also held knowledge of the past, that may encourage a deeper understanding of the historical forces that have been responsible for failures and calamities. It constitutes both an integral element of the process of 'making' citizens and a projection of the Enlightenment-derived belief that knowledge and rational analysis can improve the human condition whilst assisting the attainment of universally superior goals. This chapter gives a brief analysis of approaches and interpretations of the Second World War in the secondary education curricula of a section of European countries, as a case-study to assess the progress and the persisting flaws or stumbling blocks to a younger generation of people growing up in the reality of European integration. Recent developments in history curricula in Europe have been motivated by an increasing awareness that the 'European' perspective can be effectively accommodated within, and promoted through a constructive interaction between the national particularism and a wider 'European dimension'. This can be an invaluable resource in the mitigation of such ethnocentric narratives and in making students aware of the exciting pluralism inherent in multi-faceted comparative or thematic historical narratives that transcend the insularity of conventional perspectives on national history. But the teaching of history has acquired a new, autonomous significance in direct relation to the promotion of European citizenship amongst young people. In this sense, the scope for innovation and bold interpretations as to how historical education may fit constructively into this novel framework remains stimulatingly wide and challenging.

## Chapter Five: Becoming political in different countries

Educating for democratic citizenship requires a particular kind of citizenship education that prepares for the specific requirements of democracy. Democratic citizens-in-the-making need to acquire the knowledge, skills, and attitudes for participatory decision-making and for a way of living that respects diversity. By looking at citizenship education in different countries, one can reflect upon alternative practices and consider their consequences in varied settings. That is not to say that 'what works' in one setting will work somewhere else. Because educational practices are deeply embedded in and reflective of particular cultural contexts, they cannot be simply borrowed, but a comparative perspective enables one to see taken-for-granted practices with fresh insights and to envisage possible alternatives. This study is of citizenship education in five western democracies – the United States, England, Denmark, Germany, and the Netherlands – that share similar levels of economic prosperity, have had universal suffrage for almost a century, and have overlapping histories. They thus share similar ideals of limited government, individualism, participatory democracy, and respect for cultural diversity. At the same time, these five countries have had quite distinct traditions regarding the preparation of children and young people for their roles as citizens of democracies. I suggest that the components necessary for effective citizenship education in democracies are these: the acquisition of knowledge through planned instruction; debate about public issues; engagement in civic action; and developing positive identification with local, national, regional, and global communities. These components need to be combined in a comprehensive programme. Each element is necessary but insufficient without the others. Finally, those experiences need to be multicultural and global in nature, if we want to prepare adequately students for 21st century citizenship.

## Chapter Six: Attitudes towards European Union citizenship

The debate on European Union citizenship is discussed, by first outlining the ideas of some of the main protagonists and then analysing the way the Commission tries to find out about attitudes toward European identity and citizenship. We contrast this with the findings of research carried out with young people in London, Montpellier and Barcelona, which looked at attitudes toward issues concerning allegiance, identity and citizenship, particularly European Union citizenship. Our underlying assumptions were that, while citizenship refers to the identification of citizens with institutions, it also depends on a whole range of social attitudes connected with political participation, cultural practices, group identity and social values. This relationship between the formal aspects of citizenship and more deeply embedded allegiances means that a purely institutional approach fails to understand the deeply rooted attitudes that underlie participation (or non-participation) in political processes. Practical questions were asked, that could be understood by citizens from different countries, social classes, ethnic groups, sex and age, and that went beyond declared identification with one's country and opinions of European Union institutions, including issues such as mobility, equal opportunities, and support for multicultural policies. We found that most people feel a need to belong and are open to the idea of some kind of European identity. There was a positive attitude towards the construction of this identity, but it came more from a resigned acceptance than from active involvement. All those who live in Europe, particularly immigrants and their families, should enjoy equal rights and so feel they also belong: this was seen as important in terms of social cohesion. Educators should give new kinds of civics classes, which should abandon the search for common history and moving away from the defence of cultural patrimony, and instead be based firstly on teaching how to accept people at their face value, and secondly on an institutionalised rights-based polity at the EU level. This could reinvigorate the democratic process and lead to the creation of a strong democratic allegiance. The aim would be to achieve the seemingly impossible feat of finding the basis of a European identity that engages and has meaning for all its citizens.

## Chapter Seven: The social and political learning needs of refugee students and asylum seekers from Third World Countries in Irish post-primary schools

This qualitative study investigates the educational provision for refugee students in Ireland at post-primary level with particular regard to their social and political learning needs. The group of students investigated arrived in Ireland during the previous three years from African or Asian countries and they are currently attending courses in a Dublin college. Their social and political needs were assessed, based on their perceptions of their lives in Dublin and the problems they experience in their daily lives in the city. Students' experiences centred on three main areas of concern: their feelings of social exclusion and discrimination; their problems dealings with officialdom and their views on the political system; and their hopes and aspirations for the future. Although the refugees were positive in their assessments of the range of educational provision they were very concerned about the discrimination they experienced in their daily lives and their continued exclusion. Although they welcomed the security of their new lives, they felt demeaned and singled out in their dealing with officials. Their expectations for the future were based on their avowed aim to study and avail themselves of every educational opportunity. These findings are indicative of a lack of provision for a course specially designed to meet the social and political learning needs of refugees at post-primary levels. This provision could usefully be complemented by parallel in-service training for those officials of the state dealing in their professional capacity with refugees.

## Chapter Eight: Young people, citizenship and politics in Europe today

The political situation that newly characterises the European countries are well known: the crisis of the State, the loss of credit from which both politicians and political parties are suffering, the slump in traditional indirect participation, the confusion of the sense of territorial belonging, and a fully-open debate about universalism (vs. particularism). Some oft-cited theories are recalled. Differences between countries are briefly mentioned, followed by age-related variations. The second part of the chapter focuses on the results of two complementary surveys, carried out with comparable panels of young French students (age 18–25) and addressing the perception of politics and citizenship. The notion of citizenship is disconnected from the sphere of politics that is burdened with disparaging associations.

## Chapter Nine: The introduction of the euro as a means to create a new feeling of territorial belonging

The chapter studies political socialisation via the introduction of the euro in the twelve countries of the European Monetary Union. Teenagers' attitudes toward the euro and its social representations are examined before 2002 and after. Data concerning the influence of the euro in relation to becoming more European are discussed. Two samples of teenagers (11- to 18-year-olds) were interviewed over two distinct periods: (i) six months before the introduction of the euro and (ii) during the first months after the euro notes and coins replaced the national currency. The results obtained from the two samples over these two phases do not reveal a complete change in attitude among the subjects. When the euro was still virtual, the overall attitude towards it appeared neutral, as if the subjects did not care about the new currency. Once the euro arrived, our teenagers did not seem as enthusiastic as the adult population but do have a more positive attitude than before. The differences for each sample are considered over the two periods of the study; in the second phase, subjects' attitudes and representations are also compared according to gender. In terms of the influence of the euro in becoming more European, there has been a significant change in the overall feeling of belonging; this feeling is analysed and discussed.

## Chapter Ten: European values and political education

This overview focuses on the results of the three EVS surveys (1981, 1990 and 1999–2000), the last covering more than half a billion Europeans. It is striking that 'tolerance' has become steadily more important, a value much needed for our multicultural and multi-religious society. But tolerance has a double meaning, positive as well as negative: while we can and should tolerate the existence of different religions, we should not tolerate the oppression of women by religion; we can and should tolerate a plurality of political parties, but we have to be intolerant regarding the people who deny the Holocaust and the concentration camps. People who are tolerating such denial are undermining democracy by a culture of dishonesty and lies. Tolerance means pluralism. And pluralism is a consequence of individualisation, a process that characterises more and more the European state of mind. However, individualisation doesn't automatically mean individualism. In *The Good Society* Bellah (1992) stresses that society relies on institutions and he mentions among them the market and organised work, the government, the law and the Churches. The European Union might be added to his list of institutions. In our surveys Europeans have more confidence in the European Union than in their own national parliaments. Which means that for them, Europe is a symbol of hope, of their main values of freedom, equality and solidarity. It is on this hope that a solid education project can be built. Convinced, after the disaster of the Second World War, that one had to try the impossible, Monnet, Schuman, Adenauer, de Gasperi and later many other great leaders have been inspired by this realistic utopia. It is this vision which should be in the mind of every teacher.

# 1

# Introduction:
# Growing up politically
# in Europe today

## Alistair Ross and
## Christine Roland-Lévy

This book is concerned with young people's political learning in contemporary Europe. Some initial definitions of this focus may be useful: we will justify these in the arguments that follow. By young people, we are referring to the period from birth to adulthood, because political learning starts young and carries on: although it is obviously a life-long learning process, we chose to focus on the earlier stages. 'Political learning' in this context means all the ways, formal and informal, by which these young members of society come to understand the rules, processes, institutions and patterns of behaviour that relate to the way in which societies organise themselves, allocate values and resources, and create and execute rules. The reference to 'contemporary' refers particularly to the period that is current for young people (which is rather shorter and more immediate than what is 'current' for older people), and we use 'Europe' in a loose cultural sense, not in a legalistic or formal sense. The central threads running through the various chapters in this book will amplify, explain and justify these definitions and qualifications. Our concerns are both with political socialisation and with political education.

Although an individual's identity can be seen as fluid and contingent, changing and responding to context and to personal and wider history, it is also initially and most powerfully formed in the early years of the individual's life. The identity – or identities – of a young adult are by no means immutable, but have already been formulated and expressed. Various aspects of identity develop between birth and adulthood: the sequence of construction is itself contingent on the social and political circumstances in which the individual grows up. Some of these aspects of identity are undoubtedly concerned with a *political* identity. They will include, *inter alia*, aspects of identity that relate to particular geographical localities (such as municipalities, nations and regions), as well as aspects that relate to membership of a particular social group that may act politically (for example, a socio-economic class, a linguistic group, or a particular ethnicity). There are some important consequences of this kind of identity. Firstly, they will frequently overlap – a Basque-speaking working-class resident of Spain, for example – and each individual will have to decide, in any particular locality, time and context, whether these identities can be mutually compatible or whether one or two over-ride the others. Political participation will depend on this. Secondly, most of these forms of political identity are defined in relation to the other: to have such an identity necessarily excludes other who do not have this identity. We can see this through European history: the distinction made between Roman citizen and non-citizen, between Greek and Barbarian, between Jew and Gentile, between Aryan and non-Aryan – in each case a definition created by a member of the former group, rather than one of the latter.

Such distinctions and discriminations define the identity of the individual within the group and the group itself. They begin to be developed early in life. Before they reach their teens, most children know the nationality to which they 'belong', as well as their social class: many also know their sectarian, linguistic, ethnic and other allegiances. They will also be learning how to behave towards those with different political identities.

But the situation in which learning takes place is no longer stable and the context is rather different from the context in which their parents and teachers passed through the same stages. The experiences of successive generations have differed throughout modern times but, as Edye demonstrates in Chapter 6, the pace of change has vastly accelerated. In Chapter 10, Kerkofs refers to the rapid development in politico-social values in the world and across Europe in particular. He points out that while most parents are 'still primarily rooted in the small territory of the village or town', this is not true of their children. Not only are there new boundaries, and new states, but the very nature of a boundary and a state is shifting in the new politics of Europe. Autonomies and hegemonies that had seemed as fixed as Aristotelian crystal spheres are now seen to be in motion.

Identity and citizenship are not coterminous, but have elements that are linked. Linda Colley writes that identity is 'ancestral and visceral', while citizenship is 'political and functional' (1999), but it is more complex than this on the European stage. As Feertchak notes in Chapter 9, there are fundamental differences between *jus sanguinis* and *jus solius* – citizenship based on descent (as, until very recently, an element of the German conception of the *staatsbürger*) is very different from that based on territory. There are difficulties in translation of the term – Germans also have *stadtsbürger*, the town-citizen, while *staatsbürger* could be translated as state citizen; but neither have the specific territoriality that is contained within the French *citoyenitee*, and a *cittadino* may mean something else. Citizenship itself is a word that is contingent: to the Estonian, it is a concept that may be used to discuss the presence of a large Russian minority within Estonian boundaries; to the asylum seeker it may mean a legal status that brings safely and permanence, to the French it is a territorial attachment (that may not be as enduring as it seems – the integral home territory, not so long ago, included what is now Algeria), and to many Belgians, citizenship is already plural – a residual Belgian citizenship being little more than a flag of convenience, compared to the much stronger provincial affinities.

Citizenship and political education are necessarily contentious areas. Politics is about how resources and values are authoritatively

3

allocated in society when power is unevenly distributed. This inevitably means balancing the relationships between the various needs of different individuals with the polity, when each individual has developed their own, increasingly kaleidoscopic, identity in relationship to society and the body politic. When individuals chose to identify themselves contingently – behaving as a members of one set of cross-cutting groups in one context, and as a member of different groupings in another – then allegiances to political institutions will also become variable: indeed, the institutions themselves will become more transient, multi-dimensional and potentially fragmentary in response to this complexity of the individual identity. Such traditional political concepts as rights and duties, representation, freedom and justice become problematised (but not in any sense less important) because of this. The idea of multiple identities is now common: indeed, Edye (Chapter 6) suggests that most young people are 'more or less comfortable with a notion of multiple identity as a form of self-definition'.

To give an example: a young bilingual teenager of Turkish and German parentage and living in Germany, may at times identify herself by her religion (and use in this context a particular set of obligations, and a particular moral code from among the wide range of patterns of practice and belief encompassed within the overall term 'Muslim'), at other times see herself as a young woman in a particular western culture, which will involve appreciating certain sorts of pop music, dress and behaviour, and at other times with identities that may centre either on her 'German-ness', her 'Turkishness', or her combination of the two, or on either of her two language communities (neither of which is simply coterminous with Germany or Turkey), or her identity as an individual who can operate in both languages. This list by no means completes the possible reference groups that this – not at all unusual – thirteen-year-old may have. And each of these reference groups brings with it different sets of duties and obligations, and different definitions of whom she will include in the reference group and who falls outside it. She will expect different rights from the various groups and from the individuals in those groups, and she will have and expect different degrees of participation in decision-making processes in each setting. She will inevitably find that some of these demands are sometimes incompatible and will have to give priority, in a particular setting, to acting in one way or another: she will live contingently. Moreover, her decisions in this respect may well be unique: neither she nor we can expect another young bilingual Turkish-German girl in the same town to make the same decisions about her identity. Edye points out that such multiplicities are particularly important to the many Europeans of mixed descent and Kileavy, in Chapter 7, notes that provision for them is particularly needed in those parts of Europe that have only recently begun attracting migrants.

Such a young woman is not unusual among the many millions of young people in contemporary Europe, and they are growing in number. The mobility that is encouraged by the European Union, the region's need for migrants and the globalisation of work and employment make it highly probable that patterns such as these will become the norm in the next half century. We need to ask what this means for our patterns of education, and particularly our citizenship or political education. What skills will this young woman need to participate in social and political events? What understandings will she need about different and sometimes conflicting institutions, value systems and beliefs? What social attitudes and procedural concepts will enable her to negotiate her life, to make judgements about social risks and opportunities, to participate in controlling her society? The answers to these questions are not simple but we can say that they will not be achieved by the simple civic education of the past – being a good German, a good Turk, or even a good European.

Benedict Anderson argued that our national communities are imaginary. By this he meant the reality of a modern nation-state existed primarily in the shared imagination of its members, that we construct ourselves as good members of our national community through holding a shared picture that represents a linked history,

5

language, culture and identity. 'Europe' is as much a mutual imaginary icon as are each of our individual nations. Norman Davies' history of Europe emphasises this: Europe in any objective description is no more that the extreme end of the great Eurasian landmass. But what we mean when we use the term Europe is some sense of collective bond, some shared culture, history, set of values. However, when it comes to definition, we can no more define what is shared than we can delimit the geography. Europe for many years was used to mean what we now call Western Europe, with a fragile and indeterminate eastern boundary – this might be the Vistula, or the Dneiper, or the Don, or the Volga, or the Urals. Stradling (2001) points to the divergence between those who define Europe by its shared cultural heritage, and those who emphasise its diversity. The former stress Graeco-Roman philosophy and Judaeo-Christian ethics and beliefs and focus on shared historical experiences – the Crusades, feudalism, the Enlightenment – while the latter highlight the variety of ethnic and linguistic groups, the shared loyalties, conflicts, nationalisms and the political and economic dynamics that arise from fragmented, rather than centralised, power. There are, as Kallis illustrates in his analysis of textbooks on the 1939–45 war in Chapter 4, horizontal, transnational bonds that unite the continent which run concurrently with vertical particularist nationalisms. Today, Europe is often used as a synonym for the European Community: one of us recently heard a Latvian complain that when he arrived at immigration in Brussels or Paris he was often asked 'And how long do you intend to stay in Europe?' To which he tried to answer 'I hope I'll carry on doing so for the rest of my life.' Various parts of Europe detach themselves: Boystov observes that Russians simultaneously conceive of themselves as mainly Europeans, while referring to Europe as the other. Inhabitants of the United Kingdom and of Ireland have until relatively recently used Europe as a term for the Continent, from which they were semi-detached. One (apocryphal) London newspaper headline from the early 20th century sums this up: 'Fog in the Channel: Europe cut off'.

The Europe of this book is perhaps more distinct, but nevertheless still not defined. We certainly include all the members of the European Union, the European Economic Area and the Accession states that are seeking to join the Union. And beyond this, Switzerland, Croatia, Bosnia … and the Ukraine, Belarus, Moldavia, Georgia … and Russia itself? What of Israel (a longstanding contributor to the Eurovision Song Contest)? And if Israel, why not Palestine? Where does Europe end?

Perhaps it is not surprising that in such situations we can detect some hesitation in the relationship between electorates and the elected. It is argued that there is increasing political alienation and apathy, and that many voters in many European countries appear less inclined to participate in electoral systems. There has been much concern about the 'democratic deficit' that appears to be widening in election after election. It is also claimed that the younger cohorts of voters are even more disinclined to participate than their parents are, although this is disputed, even within this volume: while Edye in Chapter 5, and Feertchak in Chapter 8 both refer to a decline in participation in electoral activity by the young, Davies and Thorpe in Chapter 3 suggest that there is no evidence of a generational decline in voter turnout. Such arguments are based on a particular view of what constitutes political participation in a democracy (Borhaug, 1999). The notion of the civic culture, as developed by (largely) American political scientists in the early decades of the Cold War period, conceived of the active citizen as an occasional, but infrequent, participant in elections, with long intermitting periods of political quiescence (Almond and Verba, 1965). Whether such a view of 'political activity' was ever accurate is debatable: it certainly appears alien in the social and political activism of many people today. The fragmentary identities we have referred to cannot be effectively catered for by umbrella political organisations or rainbow coalitions, nor can infrequent elections for political institutions that no longer have the sovereignty, autonomy and independence that were found in simpler times. The sovereignty of institutions has been an inevitable casualty of the interdependence of the global society. The *polis* no longer has the simplicity (or the inequality) of the Athenian city-state.

There is in all this a need to display a certain caution at the cries of politicians and bureaucracies about the growth in political alienation: there are signs of what Cohen called 'moral panic' here. It is worth remembering that the identity of the politician and the civil servant is inherently defined by the existence of the political institutions and frameworks in which they work. As Ross points out in Chapter 2, declining to participate in electoral structures – for whatever reason – undermines the legitimacy of their office and their identity. Cries for increased political education may at least in part be demands to be authenticated through the ballot box. Politicians need the electorate to confirm the politicians' identity, more than the electorate need the politicians to articulate the electorate's identity.

But this is not to deny that these changes in identity, authority and sovereignty do not also have an important effect on traditional politics. Contingency and more transient identities and allegiance also produce, among a sizeable minority of people, young and old, a yearning for the certainty of more simple political hegemonies, and xenophobic and racist movements often have their origins in a desire to return to a time that may be mythical or imagined (*pace* Anderson) of the certainties of a united, monoethnic, monoglot society.

The implications of this for political and citizenship education are correspondingly far-reaching. We know that political learning starts at an early age. Easton and Dennis (1969) gave the example of a four-year-old child in a car whose parent was stopped by the police for speeding. Hitherto the child had lived in a world where all adults exercised power over all children: now came a realisation that the world was not so simple and that some adults had power over other adults. The hierarchies of power and authority are part of early learning, as is the distinction between power and authority.

Every night television series demonstrate that those in authority – the nation, its police and its armed services – have the authority and right to use force, often violent force, while the use of power by those not in authority is illegitimate and destined to failure.

We also create an ethos of power and authority structures in our schools and educational settings. The nature of many schools is that the teacher is expected to be the authoritative source of knowledge and the distributor of justice, rules and regulations that can appear arbitrary and imposed. Hahn shows in Chapter 5 how common this form of schooling is, and that the occasional example of a more democratically organised *Folkskole* only goes to demonstrate the prevalence of the rule. Most schooling systems are structured to reinforce systems of authority and control: indeed, some sociologists such as Stan Bowles and Herb Gintis (1976) have argued that in a capitalist society, schools were *designed* to instil conformity to the authority of work patterns, making children compliant and uncritically accepting of authority. But despite the tension between the role of the teacher educator and the autonomy of the learner, it is possible to develop systems in schools which accord children rights and responsibilities in decision making. Pedagogic authority can be distinguished from organisational power structures (see, for example, the Summerhill system – Titchiner, 2001). If schools are authoritarian structures, can we expect much practical citizenship education within them?

This is the third volume in the series *European Issues in Children's Identity and Citizenship*, which has been developed by the Children's Identity and Citizenship (CiCe) Thematic Network. The Network, supported as part of the European Commission's ERASMUS programme since 1998, brings together many people with an academic and professional interest in political learning. This volume is the central one of a projected trilogy within the series – *Understanding of Economic Issues* was published in 2002, and we plan to add a volume on learning about society. We drew the contributors to this book from both within and without the Network, and each was asked to identify a major dimension as a basis from

9

which to examine political learning in Europe today. Most contributors use examples of contemporary research to illustrate a synoptic overview of the issues, thus providing some descriptive depth to illuminate the broader points.

We begin with some examples of current **policy and practice** in the field. Drawing on experiences with younger children (Ross) and with older pupils (Davies and Thorpe), Chapters 2 and 3 explore the processes for handling political issues in the classroom. Ross distinguishes different curricular traditions, based respectively on concepts, experience and issues. He argues that each has particular advantages and drawbacks, and that teachers are most effective in political education when they create a synthesis, in which children construct conceptual ideas that bring together experiential knowledge and issue-based information. The role of the teacher in managing the discussion process is critical in this, particularly when, as is inevitable in political education, children are asked to handle disputes and controversies about the distribution of power, justice and values.

Davies and Thorpe advance this further, identifying particular procedural values – rationality and critical appreciation of the contemporary, tolerance and pluralism, participation, acceptance of responsibilities and appreciation of rights. Given the contested nature of citizenship and identity, developed earlier in this chapter, such procedural values should clearly be located at the core of current learning about identity and citizenship. Our hypothetical Turkish-German thirteen-year-old girl will need to apply models of rationality to understand how her own identity is only partially congruent with that of her peers: this will call for tolerance on her part and for a decision on the political arenas and discourses in which she will participate. She'll also need to recognise that her responsibilities will sometimes be dependent on the identities she adopts – for example, expectations of her as a Muslim may be different from those of her as a girl among her classroom peers. Equally, while she should undoubtedly enjoy fundamental human rights, other rights will be contingent on the community in which she operates, and the identity she elects to adopt within this community. Tolerance of diversity and pluralism are the underling procedural concepts that she (and her peers) will need, and the role of teachers and others in sensitively fostering this and related values, through developing confidence and respect for others, is critical.

Davies and Thorpe set these procedural values within the context of traditional curriculum areas in England that might be expected or able best to 'deliver' a political education, and examine the respective merits and limitations afforded by History, Language and Personal and Social Education. Teaching history, in particular, they identify as a potential 'training ground for toleration', and it is also a particular facet of historical education that is at the centre of Kallis's case study in Chapter 4. The contested nature of a European identity is brought to the fore in this analysis of representations of the Second World War in different national curricula. Kallis looks at how various national accounts have been successively revised and represented, comparing how differently some vertical and particularist national accounts of the period have been modified to incorporate broader-based horizontal accounts. Nevertheless, he warns, the ethnocentric legacy persists, and much of the history that is taught about the post-war period claims that cooperation in Europe has *led* to a sense of historical and cultural affinity, and not that such a sense of affinity has been the underlying *cause* of the cooperation. The legacy of these interpretations of the war thus contaminates our understanding of European collaboration. Kallis identifies three persistent ethnocentricities in current school texts: attempts to 'redeem' the nation by emphasising particular forms of resistance and liberation; extolling the nation through focusing on participation in the Allied cause or in resistance to the Axis cause; and attempts to specify the nation as distinct from 'the other'.

How important is curriculum history in the creation of national – and other – identities? Kallis argues that is an essential constituent in the making of citizens and the construction of individual and group identity. It 'holds the key to a constructive dialectical relation between memory, present experience and future expectations'. A contrary view has recently been expressed by Ahonen (2001), who examines Finnish teenagers' memories of the past as a constituent of their current identities, and concludes that their effective family memory of the past is confined to just three generations. In this analysis, the memories of grandparents of today's teenagers are largely post-world war. Perhaps at last the nationalistic accounts of the wars of twentieth century in Europe will begin to fade – though not in the Balkans for a further fifty years.

There are other histories being presented, which do take on the horizontal dimensions of Europe. Norman Davies' books *Europe: A History* (1997) and its mirror work on Britain and Ireland, *The Isles* (1999)) are examples at the level of text, but there have also been substantial re-presentations of Europe in exhibitions that have, for example, emphasised the transnational: museum displays that take up themes of Neolithic Europe, Celtic Europe, Renaissance Europe and Enlightenment Europe that focus on the commonalties and ubiquity of these cultures.

Hahn in Chapter 5 describes a rather different curriculum element. Countries and contexts matter in political learning: there may be transnational and global factors that influence how young people become political, but there are also unique aspects that arise from local historic, philosophic and cultural traditions. The curriculum elements that she identifies as essential for citizenship education, though differently described, resonate with those suggested by Ross, Davies and Thorpe: Hahn argues for 'carefully planned instruction', followed by deliberation about public issues, engagement in civic action and positive identification with different communities, from the local to the global. Civic identity, constructed from young people's discourse with their family, peers, media and culture, will be culturally specific, but there is also in common across the states in the study a high level of participation, debate and action. In particular, she describes the growth of 'service education', in which young people are encouraged to develop responsibility towards others through community service. This is sometimes seen as a programme of citizenship education that is sufficient in itself – volunteering to help in the community can, however, be an effective way of opting out of political education. As Hahn emphasises, such volunteering must be combined as a part of comprehensive programme that includes the other elements of instruction, debate and tolerance of identity. Service learning can lead to passive citizenship, and the 'voting and volunteering' outcomes of a traditionalist process of political learning can be severely limiting and disabling, and ultimately exclude citizens from real participation and engagement.

The next chapters set political education today in the political context. In Chapter 6 Edye takes up Hahn's identification of contingent factors in different national settings. He contrasts the findings of the large scale quantitative surveys of young people's opinions across Europe – Eurobarometer and the Continuous Tracking Survey – with much richer qualitative data derived from interviews with young people in three strategic locations, representing north European scepticism, founding member doubts, and southern pro-integration. Young people's views of citizenship and allegiance, he suggests, are complex and multiple. Resigned acceptance of a European identity is coupled with the need for cultural and social cohesion, and emotional attachment to a sense of territory. At the same time, European citizenship is viewed as a right, with positive instrumental benefits, a strong feeling of solidarity for minority and immigrant groups, and the desire that they be given full rights of citizenship. These attitudes are receiving some attention at the level of the European Union, for example though the beginnings of a rights-based policy adopted at the Nice summit in 2000, and the development of the Union's White Papers in 2001 on *European Governance – A White Paper* (COM (2001) 428) and *A New Impetus for Youth* (COM (2001) 681). If effective, these policies would begin to address the sense of apathy and resignation that Edye detects, and to challenge the fairly instrumental attitude that he describe young people as having towards Europe. However, on one matter the young people appear ahead of the politicians. He describes 'strong expressions of solidarity for immigrant groups', who should be 'accorded full rights, including voting rights'.

The rights of minorities and migrants – including their right to citizenship education – is addressed by Killeavy in Chapter 7. Ireland, for centuries a country that provided emigrants for the world labour market, has lately become a country of net immigration. This follows a pattern already developing in the Scandinavian countries, and one that is well-established in the Netherlands, the UK, France and Germany. The combination of prosperity and an increasingly ageing population mean that Europe as a whole will be a net importer of economic migrants over the next half century, so the issues Killeavy raises are particularly timely for all Europe. Refugee and immigrant children and young people will need education and particularly need citizenship education, and the host population will need education in the procedural concepts of tolerance and understanding of diversity. One of the key tests for any system that describes itself as democratic is how it deals with people at the margins of society, particularly those whose inclusion as citizens appears most in doubt – minorities, migrants, refugees, the dispossessed, the homeless and the vagrant. How our educational systems teach young people to include everyone will be a critical challenge for political and citizenship educators everywhere.

There are other major political changes at work in Europe: how do these affect the political participation and understanding of young people? Feertchak in Chapter 8 uses a wide variety of sources – including both Eurobarometer and the European Values Survey – which Kerkhofs describes more fully in Chapter 10 – to pick out changes in universalism and particularism. Despite the variety of political cultures to be found in Europe, ranging from the egalitarian to the individualistic, with affiliation variously by descent or by residence, she finds a remarkably even pattern across the states she surveys. Young people are identifying increasingly with being citizens of the world, rather than of a particularism. Despite the level of non-participation in elections, fewer young people, she argues, remain unpoliticised – but they are deeply suspicious of politics.

Another of the changing aspects of European politics and identity is found in the monetary system. One of the critical concepts in national identity has been the currency. Not for nothing did Emperors and Kings portray their head on the coins and specie of the world: this was an effective form of propaganda demonstrating the extent and ubiquity of their power. We now have a new currency across much of Europe, the Euro, with its own distinctive icon joining the rare group of internationally recognised icons – this time a distinctively homegrown symbol. Roland-Lévy (Chapter 9) explores how young people in France responded to the change, and whether or not it changes their conception of 'being European'. Her principal finding – that the economic and political change has brought about a 'specific fundamental modification in terms of political socialisation' – is significant. Territorial belonging has appreciably weakened amongst young people and this is bringing about 'an entirely new European feeling of belonging'. This would suggest that we are witnessing as profound a change as occurred at the birth of the modern nation states. Just as Colley argued that one of the foundations of the sense of being British was manufactured or forged in the early eighteenth century through a sense of mercantilism (1992), so the new trading of the European monetary area seems to be a fundamental prop of the idea of a common European identity.

The European Values Survey was initiated by a small group of academics nearly a quarter of a century ago: one of them, Jan Kerkhofs, returns to review all three surveys in Chapter 10. The **Values and Context** of change in Europe constitute our final section. The strengths of a longitudinal study are apparent, as Kerkhofs is able to unpick the developing sense of tolerance across Europe, and the development of pluralism. It might be particularly apposite here to remind particularly British readers of this chapter to themselves be tolerant of the discourse of a Belgian writer in English: Kerkhofs' use of terms such as black genes and genetic mutations, which may grate on the ears of the politically correct, but are delivered in a spirit of tolerance and welcoming of the changing populations of Europe. As he notes, there are important inter-generational differences apparent here, and young people's socialisation may be quite different from that of their parents and even more so their grandparents.

The overall theme of this volume is young people's political learning in contemporary Europe. Its chapters show that we are looking at a new political education: the changes are occasioned partly by political, social and economic change – as always, but at an increasing pace – and partly by an emerging new kind of 'territory' – part geographical, but more a territory of the shared collective mind. Europe is developing as a shared set of mental values that gave the potential to develop as much a sense of shared identity as did the old nationalisms of the nineteenth century. This will demand new educational structures and forms: this volume hope to contribute by setting out some of the issues and agendas.

# 2

# Children's Political Learning: Concept-based approaches versus Issues-based approaches

Alistair Ross

Political education is not a term in frequent use today: for many years it has been regarded with suspicion. In much of Eastern Europe it is now associated with the educational policies of the former regimes as something akin to indoctrination. In Western Europe and North America, it has been respectively criticised as impossible, unnecessary and an interference with the liberties of the individual and/or family. It has been argued that children are incapable of social thinking of the complexity needed to understand politics; that political understanding should not be formally transmitted by the educational system but should properly be absorbed from family, the media and the political institutions themselves, and that political education is impossible to tackle in an unbiased, even-handed way, and should therefore not be attempted. Despite all these criticisms, recent years have seen a resurgence of interest in the area, often through various forms of 'rebranding' as civics education, citizenship education, or political literacy. This chapter has two foci: a critique of current initiatives and, secondly, some examination of current practice with younger children, identifying particular problems displayed by different contemporary models of political education.

## The development of political education: a UK perspective

There was some incipient interest in political education in UK primary education in the late 1960s and early 1970s, largely as part of the political literacy movement of that time, developed by the Politics Association. Bernard Crick at Birkbeck College, London and Ian Lister at the University of York, attempted with some success to challenge the traditional teaching of Government and Politics in the secondary school. Up to then, these subjects had been dominated by teaching about structures and formal procedures, such as details of the various stages of the passage of a Bill through Parliament, and the precise functions of Black Rod. Crick and Lister (1978) proposed that secondary school children all needed to become politically literate, by which they meant to develop the skills to evaluate political discussion and make informed judgements about political alternatives. Through a series of discussion papers Crick (1974) developed a matrix of core concepts, which, he maintained, encompassed a far better reality of political activity than the sterile learning of structures.

| Government | Power | Authority | Force | Order |
|---|---|---|---|---|
| Relationship between government and society | Law | Justice | Representation | Pressure |
| Society | Natural rights | Individuality | Freedom | Welfare |

Some of these ideas were taken up by teachers of younger children, and through the 1970s there were a number of descriptions of primary school children's activities that seemed to develop political understanding (Margerison, 1968, 1972; Riches, 1974; Robins and Robins, 1978; Wagstaff, 1978; Ross, 1981). These activities were varied, and are discussed more fully later in this chapter. They included having children role-play decision-making about difficult situations – on a deserted island, for example, where they had to make and enforce their own rules; discussions of authority and power in local decisions; and drawing parallels between political fables such as *Animal Farm* (Orwell, 1943) and *Watership Down* (Adams, 1969) and human politics. These activities were discreetly encouraged by HMI (government school inspectors): the authors of the political education section in *A View of the Curriculum* (DES, 1980b), for example, and in particular the Senior Staff Inspector for History, John Slater, were particularly supportive.

The 1980s were, in contrast, a period in which any form of teaching about society, let alone politics, was officially discouraged by the Government and its agents of curriculum development and control. By the time of the National Curriculum, only the most traditional subjects were to be taught, and in a tightly controlled manner. For example, the subject of History – the remaining subject most consonant with the development of political ideas – had to be taught on the basis that school history came to an end 25 years before the present day, and parallels with contemporary society were prohibited. In the primary school, learning about society was curtailed, even in its broadest terms, except inasmuch that children were encouraged to learn about the economic foundations of society. The Secretary of State for Education, Sir Keith Joseph, once enumerated what these foundations were: 'some understanding of such matters as the operation of supply and demand, price, quality, profit and loss, competition and monopoly; such aspects as the creation of the nation's private and public wealth, customer satisfaction, enterprise, management and productivity and taxation' (1985, quoted in SCDC/EEA, 1987).

There was some slight room for manoeuvre left in what were called the cross curricular themes that were expected to permeate the formal curriculum subjects. These were citizenship, environmental, careers education, economic and industrial understanding and health education. *Curriculum Guidance 6, Citizenship Education*, (NCC, 1990) set out a singularly insipid set of suggestions for developing concepts of duties and rights. For many decades up to the 1980s, the two had been described in the order 'rights and duties', and this represented an important point of liberty: the rights of the citizen were seen as being independent of and antecedent to any duties. Only in extreme cases were some rights forfeited. Keith Joseph first made this reversal in 1985, when he talked of 'duties and rights', and distinct political points were made by the Conservative government over the next few years about the duty of the citizen and the role of the private sector (see Heater, 1990, for example). The emphasis on the responsibilities that the citizen owed the state was kept up through the following decade – there was a book of some influence, *The Principle of Duty* by David Selbourne (1994). The cross curricular themes were downgraded as successive Secretaries of State for Education promoted the core and foundation subjects, until there no place was left for any learning that concerned how society worked (Ahier and Ross, 1994).

## Citizenship Education in the UK and Europe in the late 1990s

New Labour maintained many of the previous Government's policies: in education in particular it emphasised that it was not interested in adjusting the structures of the curriculum, or of educational provision and administration, and was focusing on 'standards' (Blair, 1997). Nevertheless, there was a scheduled review of the National Curriculum, and it had already been signalled that this was to include elements of citizenship education. A working party was established to consider this, chaired by Bernard Crick, and resulted in a formal new foundation subject for Citizenship – to be mandatory in secondary schools, and to be recommended in primary schools, from September 2002. There are some disappointing features about this. For example, the Secretary of State's introduction refers to 'roles and responsibilities as citizens' (Blunkett, p. 3). Only deep in the proposals themselves are we are told that pupils must understand 'the rights ... of citizens' (p. 31).

There have been parallel moves in the context of the European Union. In *Towards a Europe of Knowledge* (COM (97) 563), the former Commissioner for Education and Youth, Edith Cresson, called for 'the achievement of citizenship through the sharing of common values, and the development of a sense of belonging to a common social and cultural area ... a broader-base understanding of citizenship founded on mutual understanding of the cultural diversities that constitute Europe's originality and richness'. There has been a series of initiatives designed to improve the understanding of European political institutions, calls for European citizenship, and initiatives to foster democratic understanding amongst young people.

> Our education programmes should encourage all young Europeans to see themselves not only as citizens of their own regions and countries, but also as citizens of Europe and the wider world. All young Europeans should be helped to acquire a willingness and ability to preserve and promote democracy, human rights and fundamental freedoms.
>
> *Council of Europe*, Recommendation R (83) 4 of the Committee of Ministers Concerning the Promotion of an Awareness of Europe in Secondary Schools, 1983.

> The European dimension in Education should strengthen in young people a sense of European identity and make clear to them the value of European civilisation.
>
> *Council and the Ministers of Education*, 24 May 1988.

> Citizenship of the Union is hereby established.
>
> Article 8, *Treaty on European Union*, Maastricht, 7 February 1992.

> Education systems should educate for citizenship; and here Europe is not a dimension which replaces others, but one that enhances them. Education for citizenship should include experiencing the European dimension and socialisation in a European context because this enables each citizen to play a part on the European stage. Teachers should develop a European perspective alongside national and regional allegiences; to make use of the shared cultural heritage; to overcome cultural and lingustic obstacles.
>
> *Green Paper on the European Dimension in Education*, 29 September 1993.

The objectives of the Socrates programme include: 'to develop the European dimension in education at all levels so as to strengthen the spirit of European citizenship' (Socrates *Guidelines for Applicants*, 1996, Erasmus p. 6).

## Some problems with the concept of citizenship

However, many educators in contemporary Europe approach the concept of European identity with some caution. While there is some enthusiasm for working in the area of European citizenship, this embraces a rather different conception to those outlined by the various Councils of Ministers and treaties. Any new notion of citizenship or identity based on the new Europe must be distinctly different from the old citizenships of the nation-states: less ethno-centric, more diverse, more inclusive, less wedded to nationalistic conceptions. Osler (1994), for example, urges caution, and the 'development of an inclusive rather than an exclusive understanding of identity and citizenship'. Similar qualifications are made by Clough, Menter and Tarr, in their analysis of developing citizenship education in Latvia (1995): they suggest inclusivity rather than equality as a core concept, arguing that citizenship needs in plural contexts to be defined in terms of 'both/and' rather than 'either/or'. Hladnik (1995) argues that European citizenship might be used in a confining manner, limited to those with a legal definition of their status, and raises the important point that refugees also should be regarded as citizens, and that our definition needs to be broad, inclusive and to be separated from historical definitions of citizenship by birth, ancestry or naturalisation.

The European programmes make much of the ideas of nested identities, and seek to promote citizenship at European level as part of a self-identity that includes national and regional elements. The *Qualification and Curriculum Authority*, QCA, Citizenship education proposals (for England!) are perhaps understandably hazy. It is never made clear what it is that one will be educated to be a citizen. England? The United Kingdom? No: pupils must learn 'to participate in society as active citizens of our democracy'. Citizenship education 'promotes their political and economic literacy through learning about our economy and our democratic institutions, with respect for its varying national, religious and ethnic identities' (p 28). This is a most unusual sentence: note the plurality of democratic institutions, and the singularity of the 'its' – these various identities therefore seemingly refer to 'our economy'. Perhaps this is the entity of which we are citizens?

At the European level, educators have already begun to set up various programmes: their motivation, however, is not quite in accord with the European politicians. For example, the Children's Identity and Citizenship in Europe Thematic Network Project (85 European Universities, in 25 states) has members who are particularly concerned with promoting 'European citizenship' as a counter to xenophobia, racism, and what they see as a potentially problematic overemphasis on 'local' nationalism. (Ross 1999).

Both of these moves to educate for citizenship, in the UK and in Europe, have been initiated with some confusion, at the political institutional level, about identity. What are the states, or super-states, or unions, with which people identify? States themselves are not natural, but are recent social constructions, forged at the beginning of the modern period. And as a phenomenon of modernism, it is perhaps unsurprising that as the post-modernism age begins, that the legitimacy of states comes into question – both the legitimacy of individual states, and the legitimacy of states *per se*, which may be no more than *Imagined Communities* (Anderson, 1963). And these initiatives are being made when there is a very real decline in understanding, sympathy and trust in politicians and political institutions. The most recent European Parliamentary elections (June 1999) saw alarmingly low voting rates – a quarter in the UK, and less than a half in most countries in which voting is not compulsory. Why the decline? The traditional answer of the politicians – perhaps the obvious answer for them – is that there has been insufficient political education. Schools have let down the nation again: make the schools tell pupils about the virtues of democracy, and all will be well. Politicians are rightly afraid that without popular endorsement at the polls, they lack authority: getting people to vote and believe in the systems politicians stand for might restore their legitimacy. But politicians' personal identities converge with the state (or the union): much more so that the identities of most other people. Their role depends on the political entity. Questioning the existence of the nation-state, the boundaries, the rules of membership is to challenge the identity and legitimacy of the political and public services. This is a powerful motivating force for the current political emphasis on programmes for citizenship.

There are also some non-politicians who also feel themselves particularly threatened by the erosion of the idea of the nation-state. They need the authority of a state because they have identified themselves through a conception of 'their race' or their genetic stock, and they are undermined when the legitimacy of this institution is thrown into question: hence the resurgence of extreme right-wing parties across Europe. The political answer to such individuals is that they need more political education: the current rhetoric for citizenship education is, as noted earlier, interlaced with references for education to promote inclusivity and to challenge xenophobia and racism.

There is a second conceptual issue about the current focus on citizenship education: citizenship 'for democracy' is not usually well-defined. Borhaug (1999) points out that much depends on what is meant by democracy. Traditional representative democracy is achieved through the intermittent participation of the population in elections, through political parties that stand for broad principles. The key actor in representative democracy is the informed voter. The classic 1960s study of *The Civic Culture* suggested that the ideal citizen was a mixture of the active citizen and the passive subject (and suggested that the leading exponent of this tradition was Britain) (Almond and Verba, 1965). But there are other kinds of democratic action, and many people over the past two decades have become involved in more specific political activities than simply supporting broad political parties. The growth of 'single issue' politics has challenged traditional politicians, who have found electors deserting mass parties in favour of pressure groups, such as various peace movements, Greenpeace, Drop the Debt and Green coalitions. The old political parties have had their activities and compromises challenged by these informed political activists. This is an alternative kind of democracy that is concerned with the issues rather than with political structures and procedures. The key actor in this form of democracy is the local activist.

But this is not what politicians and public servants want political education to be about. Their concerns are – quite naturally – with buttressing the systems and institutions that brought them into existence and maintain them in power. Politicians are concerned that citizens should understand that they have civic duties and obligations – that people should participate in political processes, understand the need for compromise, and accept the processes of decision-making. From this standpoint, if future citizens are told how the existing system is fair, how the machinery of government works in the citizens' interests, how, while interest groups must (of course) be listened to, balances need also to be struck between competing interests – then citizens will accept the legitimacy of the political processes, and become part of *The Civic Culture* – the good citizen.

## How children learn about politics

This brings the argument back to the contemporary classroom. Many primary school teachers are no longer of the view that children cannot understand political issues. Olive Stevens suggested that seven-year-olds have 'some cognitive contact with the political world': her research showed that they could see political power as 'limited, consented to and conditional upon results' (1982, p. 38; also 1979). Short points out that Piagetian notions of sequential stages of development were effectively 'dethroned' in the 1990s (1999), and suggests that our understanding of social learning has been misdirected by Piaget's analysis. Recent research in the areas of physical concepts (from which

Piaget initially derived his theories) has suggested that young children have no problems in informed discussion of abstract physical concepts (Schoulz, Saljo, *et al*, 1997).

Many descriptions of practice contribute to the analysis of how children are able to develop political understanding. Margerison (1968, 1972) described an extended project, lasting several months, in which primary school children developed an island society: as well as modelling artefacts and undertaking mapping work, there was significant emphasis on discussions used to create social and political institutions – rules, systems of justice, political debate and representative democracy. Riches (1974) worked with ten- to eleven-year-olds to develop a politically-focused programme based around a similar island theme, with discussions that made explicit links between simulated activities and contemporary political processes. Robins and Robins (1978) discuss a range of primary classroom activities that have a political focus. Wagstaff (1978) developed the *People Around Us* materials to encourage the systematic examination of eight social/political concepts through three environments that figured significantly in children's lives – the family, friendship groups and work. Ross (1981) suggested that works of children's literature could be used with classes of nine- to ten-year-olds to discuss ideas about political hierarchies, social control, and political change. Denscombe and Conway (1982) used issues in development education to examine a range of political concepts, using classroom discussion to explore issues around a conceptual framework.

These approaches share a number of characteristics. Firstly, they utilise experiences of the learners, whether direct or vicarious – role-playing, modelling, sharing a story, watching the news. Secondly, they use discussion to encourage children to articulate their ideas and to actively construct meaning from the experience. By putting together words in a social context, with their peers (and with the teacher, and adults other than teachers), a shared under-standing is achieved: these words come to express a common meaning about an experience. Thirdly, the experiences concern a specific issue, possibly controversial, that arouses opinions, dissent and disagreement. Fourthly, in these particular examples the teacher begins by identifying the concept to be developed: in each case the teacher initiates the activity because she or he intends the learners to form an abstract, transferable idea through the process.

Conceptual frameworks for learning were increasingly popular in the 1970s: Bruner's work in the *MACOS* project and Senesh's programme *Our Working World* illustrate how social, political and economic concepts were taught to children much younger than had been previously thought possible. The approach in these programmes was to build up an understanding of a concept through repeated exposure to case studies and encouraging the learner to note, discuss and mark similarities. This process led to a construction of the abstract concept. The innovation was the recognition that the abstract concept should not be taught directly as a pre-formulated definition. While it is possible to define a concept for the learner, there are a number of problems that can arise from such an approach. Firstly, most words have a variety of meanings in adult life, and contextual references are needed to establish which meaning is being employed. Concepts are fluid, and develop over time and differently in different cultures and contexts. They can be limited in their meaning if they are not recognised as generalisations and abstractions. To take but one example, 'money' has a wide variety of meanings, both in everyday life and even more so to the economist. It can mean physical change – the coins and notes we carry about with us. It also refers now to plastic credit cards and direct transfer cards. It includes deposits in our bank accounts, which are abstract savings with no tangible existence until we chose to cash them. To the economist, money is not merely a medium of exchange, but also a store of wealth, and a system to allocate value (and they employ a whole series of definitions. To teach a simple, single definition of 'money' to children is to do them a disservice: to research whether children at a particular age have the 'right' definition of money verges on the lunatic. The meanings of money are constructed by individuals, according to their particular experiences: they are not taught by definitions, and there is no 'right' understanding. The young children who say that money 'comes from shops' (or the bank, or a 'hole in the wall') are not wrong: they are simply using the concept to describe one particular meaning of money (based, quite properly, on their observations). However, to be useful, abstract concepts need to have some generally shared contextual meanings, and to develop these, we need to trade the words and to use them with references to our experiences, so that others understand them in the same way. This is why classroom discussion are needed: they allow meaning to be collaboratively constructed, not rote-learned by the individual in isolation (Bruner and Haste, 1987).

One problem that this approach can lead to is an over-emphasis of the 'issues' or of the experiential element of the learning. It is possible to teach a whole series of important social and political issues – that are engaging to the children, that are focused on their experiences and feelings, that arouse their concern – but which are not necessarily developing the construction of underlying conceptual structures or frameworks. A teacher can develop lively classroom topics on environmental issues, on issues of world poverty, of food production, of pollution, that engender lively debate, activity and emotion. These are good things in themselves: but unless there is an attempt to encourage some reflection about the principles of political behaviour that lie behind them, a valuable educational experience is lost. Children need to construct a view of adult behaviour that enables them to see the competing interests, power structures, systems of law construction and of justice, and authority systems that underpin how these issues are dealt with, and about why they *are* issues.

There is also a strong counter-ideology to such an issue-based approach. Many primary school teachers have a consensual view of the child's world, and present young children with a 'cosy' image of society that avoids controversy or references to dissent. Short (1999) draws on the work of Ronald King (in his study of an infant school significantly titled *All things bright and beautiful?* (1979))

to show how it 'was natural for teachers who believe in childhood innocence to want to protect their pupils from the harsh realities of life' (p 153). These teachers portray a consensual view of society, in which political activity and social conflict in particular is sanitised so that agreements are always reached with ease, through goodwill and consensus.

Another problem with issue-based learning approach can be the temptation to take short cuts, or to mistake the outcome for the process. Given a conceptual map, or a grouping of 'key' concepts (as in the example given above by Crick, 1974), it is possible to offer the children ready-made, hand-me-down definitions or summaries that become the 'correct' answer. This is one of the traditional techniques of the pedagogue in popular culture and experience: the teacher knows, and tells the learner what is to be known. The view of teaching as the transmission of accepted knowledge would hold that politics is a structured activity: there are known and defined institutions, there are procedures, and there are historical conventions. The way to understand politics is therefore to learn about all of these. When one has the facts, the knowledge, then one can begin to understand political activity. This traditional model, alluded to earlier, teaches the nuts and bolts of 'the constitution' rather than anything dynamic that concerns issues that are relevant to the child. Referring back to the argument made earlier in the chapter, this is the kind of political education that politicians really want to promote – an explanation of the existing system, a validation of political leaders' legitimacy, and some promotion of justice and equity. Such a view of the political system often does not match the reality of young people's experience: they are aware that despite its rhetoric, the system does not effectively address a range of social, political and economic issues that concern them – racism, poverty, the environment, housing, pollution, corruption. If teachers want to engage children in a learning process about politics, one has to start with the issues that concern them.

The solution advocated in this chapter is a delicate balance in which a variety of elements are present: experiences, issues, concepts and

29

structures and processes. It is suggested that all of these are necessary components – no single one may be left out – and that the sequence is critical.

The first stage is to select issues that are firmly grounded in pupils' direct experience. Selecting issues that can be predicted to provoke differences in the class ensures that children become engaged in talk, discussion and argument about controversial issues. Political education is thus less about structures, and more about taking on matters of concern and having a forum in which pupils can argue with each other. Issues such as poverty, homelessness, pollution, capitalism, gender, race and language are, in the writer's experience as a class teacher, very likely to lead to a sustained and pointed classroom discussion. The role of the teacher is to facilitate argument, to protect different points of view, and to be prepared to challenge the children's viewpoints. The teacher is not neutral but one who may put forward their own views, insisting however that they are only their own views, and need not be accepted by members of the class.

As a second stage, the teacher needs to map the events, processes and concepts that may arise from discussion of the issue. This planning of a programme of conceptual learning might be informed by the frameworks that Crick put forward in the 1970s: they can indicate directions in which the debates and arguments might include some of the core ideas of politics – the rule of law, representation, democracy, political rights, separation of powers, and more – and to ensure that future discussion will not just draw on these, but lead to an understanding of how these concepts relate to the issues and cases discussed. Issues-based teaching, like issues-based politics, needs a conceptual framework as a core – and in the mind of the teacher – if it is to amount to a political education. Teachers of economics would have another set of concepts, and teachers of sociology another, but all sets of concepts should be seen as heuristic devices, fluid and not to be taught as definitions.

The third stage in this sequence is to develop an initial class discussion. In this, the teacher needs to be provocative, to be a chair that allows dissent, to put forward their own view (but to maintain that it is only a view), to protects minority viewpoints, and to advocate alternative positions. This last point is perhaps the most difficult. The teacher's role is not neutral – we do not want children to be neutral on issues about which they have strong views. The teachers' intention should be to give the class a model of how to engage in political argument. They need to understand the values and procedures of political debate, such as listening to others, putting forward evidence and arguments, allowing others to differ, and picking up and elaborating points of similarity and difference. The teachers' role is more complex because they are also the chairpersons, so they also must control access to the debate, encouraging those who are quieter and more reticent, protecting the views of the minority, and so on. Another role to be combined with these is to put forward views that have not been expressed. This requires sometimes putting forward ideas that challenge the children's views – with the teacher if necessary also making it clear that they are not her or his own views – so that members of the class can respond to these, putting forward rebuttals and challenges. This may be particularly important if there is some unanimity in the class, because children need to rehearse their arguments against others who hold differing views. This can be a challenging position for the teacher.

The fourth stage is to encourage members of the class to gather information about the issue and about alternatives. This might be a return to more traditional forms of teaching, involve reference sources and library work, but it may also involve interviewing people, surveys, talking with parents and with other adults, or visits to particular locations. Meanwhile, the teacher needs to check the conceptual map: following the initial discussions, can it be predicted that the concepts originally identified will be raised? Do additional concepts need to be added?

Stage five is to re-engage in the class debate, now including the information that the children have researched. The teacher now encourages reflection and comparison, perhaps suggesting alternatives that can be used to draw out generalisations. It will be at this point that conceptual learning begins to become evident: when a child draws two events together, pointing to similarities between them, analysing commonalities and begining to make a prediction or a rule that might apply. The role of the teacher is to encourage this. The concept may only be partly formed, or may be 'wrong' in terms of an adult's definition. The teacher does not have to agree with the child's formulation, but does praise the way of thinking and endorse the process. Saying 'No, that's not right, because you've not thought of...' is likely to stop further attempts to generalise. The teacher instead considers what other information might be made available that will lead to a refinement of the concept. This can be introduced later – another child may raise some fresh evidence that challenges the generalisation, or the teacher can find a way to introduce it. The object is to get the child who first put the proposition forward to rethink it, accommodating the new information in a reformulation.

It may only be at this stage that the teacher begins to provide structural information about the processes, procedures and forms of the political system, that will enlighten and supplement the class's understanding. Voting procedure, legislative processes, officers of state, roles of legislators, rules of law and bills of rights may now be of interest and relevance. The machinery becomes more interesting and better understood when children can link it to their own experience.

This is challenging. To achieve it, teachers need a broad understanding of how structures work (not a detailed knowledge of the machinery of government); a conceptual framework on to which they can map issues as they arise; and the skill to maintain a pedagogic style that permits them *not* to know the answers, and to not be the authority.

How much can an issues-based approach be developed? If we are to get away from safe teaching about structures and processes, about the neutral and the bland, then we need to ensure that teachers are equipped with a wide conceptual understanding, with a knowledge of the issues that might illustrate these, and with the skills to manage covering the issues of participatory democracy through handling classroom political debate in ways that have not been supposed to have had a place in the classroom for a decade or more. Some preliminary investigation suggests that there is much work to be done in developing these skills (Holden, 1999).

# 3
# Thinking and acting as citizens

Ian Davies and
Tony Thorpe

This chapter explores the meaning of political literacy within citizenship education firstly by referring, generally, to a number of key issues and then, more specifically, by discussing ongoing work for a practical classroom resource based project. The review of issues in the first part of the chapter draws from debates that have taken place over the last thirty to forty years, mainly in England. The project that is discussed in the later parts of the chapter (and whose members are listed in the acknowledgements) was funded by the English Department for Education and Skills. The project had two main aims. We wanted to provide opportunities to help young people focus on what we hoped related to the essence of citizenship. We also hoped that by identifying the focus of educational work – at least in a provisional manner – to provide a platform for more meaningful professional dialogue. That dialogue would take us beyond the rhetorical phase that we have occupied for so long when debating citizenship. We want, rather ambitiously, to help move the debate from questions such as 'should we have citizenship education?' to 'what should be seen as good work in citizenship education? We describe the work of three teams within the project (Personal and Social Education, History, English) and discuss the way in which those teams have developed materials that are designed to help students become better at explaining, tolerating and participating. We refer to some practical examples from our pack of teaching materials. Finally, we draw attention to some issues that guided our evaluation of the project and by so doing suggest some of the challenges that lie ahead.

## Recent Historical Background

With some notable exceptions (e.g. see Heater, 1983) little or nothing was done in the name of political education prior to the 1960s. The little that did happen tended to be presented either in the form of courses about the British Constitution for high status academic students who were expected to go on to become leaders of society, or low status civics programmes for those who were expected to do what they were told (see also Entwistle, 1973; Batho, 1990; Davies, 1999). However, in the 1970s and also in the 1990s a remarkably similar form of political education found some sort of official legitimation. The two following quotations show this continuity:

> A politically literate person will know what the main political disputes are clearly about; what beliefs the main contestants have of them; how they are likely to affect him, and he (*sic*) will have a predisposition to try to do something about it in a manner at once effective and respectful of the sincerity of others. (Crick and Porter, 1978, p. 33).

> Pupils learning about and how to make themselves effective in public life though knowledge, skills and values – what can be called 'political literacy', seeking for a term that is wider than political knowledge alone. (QCA/DfEE, 1998, p. 13).

The similarities should not surprise us, as we know that Bernard Crick was the key figure both in the 1970s and 1990s. However, from a peak of influence in the late 1970s when leading HMIs (Government school inspectors) were writing about the importance of political competence (Slater and Hennessey, 1978) and 'the social and political' were regarded as key areas of experience until the present time, when Crick's ideas are again being welcomed, there is a curious gap. In between these surges of interest in political literacy there were, broadly, two areas of development.

Firstly, there were adventures in a large range of 'adjectival educations' (global education, peace education, antiracist education etc.) in the 1980s. These overlapping fields may not have had a great deal of overall coherence but they nevertheless probably did have an impact on teachers, with some good classroom resources being produced and many in-service programmes being managed by committed local education authority advisers (e.g. Pike and Selby, 1988). Secondly, there was, rather unfortunately, a very narrow political characterisation of citizenship education in the 1990s that saw key figures calling for young people to undertake voluntary service as way to fulfil their 'voluntary obligations'. The report of the Speaker's Commission, *Encouraging Citizenship* (Commission on Citizenship 1990), became known mainly for its promotion of 'active citizenship' in the form of young people helping others in the local community (see Davies, 1994).

Thus we are now witnessing the re-enactment of political literacy. The general absence of interest in a worthwhile political education prior to the 1970s and the diversions of the 1980s and 1990s are no longer with us. We intend in the remaining part of this chapter to explore a range of issues that may help clarify the nature of what should and will take place in the next few years as citizenship education is implemented in England. We hope that by so doing we will raise issues that may have relevance to the development of young people's understanding in other countries.

## What is Politics?

Clear distinctions need to be made (for which there is no real space in this chapter) between fundamental notions such as political indoctrination, political socialisation and political education (Harber, 1994). It is only when such distinctions are recognised that we can begin to feel some confidence that a central government sponsored citizenship curriculum would not leave schools and their students open to political manipulation and indoctrination. Further, we need to reflect on what is meant by 'politics' as we seek to provide a political education. Accordingly, we need to consider the range of possible characterisations (Cloonan and Davies, 1998) some of which are shown below:

## Contents
For some, politics is seen, variously, as a study of key circumstances (constitutional structures or events).

## Substantive concepts
This characterisation allows for an exploration of more than 'mere' content. The meaning of phenomena such as war, revolution, monarchy is investigated in order to give a much greater explicit emphasis on conceptual underpinning as opposed to a narrow concentration on events or issues.

## Perspectives
The essential nature of interpretation is acknowledged by all political scientists, although it is usually those who adopt Marxist or feminist, or post-modernist perspectives that are seen as being more explicitly committed to this emphasis. This particular focus can also include those who adopt particular approaches to the study of politics favouring, perhaps, political philosophy over the claims of other work (e.g. Horton, 1984).

## Action
This area is often rather hopelessly entangled with certain perspectives. There are those who seek to make the link between study and action in their role as public intellectuals (Goodson, 1997) with the work of Edward Said often referred to as one way of bridging the academic and the 'real' world of politics.

However, all the above fail to get behind the real nature of political literacy as intended by Crick. In 1978 he insisted that, underlying any theory of political education and any ideal of political literacy, there must be a theory of politics. Our theory of politics is much broader than many conventional views of politics – broader in two ways:

It stresses that politics is inevitably concerned with conflicts of interest and ideals, so an understanding of politics must begin with an understanding of the conflicts that there are and of the reasons and interests of the contestants: it cannot be content with pre-conceptions of constitutional order or of a necessary consensus. A politically literate person will not hope to resolve all such differences, or difficulties at once; but he (sic) perceives their very existence as politics.

It stresses the differential distribution of power there is in any society and the differential access to resources. Hence we are concentrating on a whole dimension of human experience which we characterise as political (Crick and Lister, 1978, p. 38).

It is thus important to recognise three important factors. Firstly, that a compound of knowledge, skills and procedural values is needed, with the latter to include such areas as respect for truth and reasoning and toleration, as opposed to substantive values which meant that pupils would be told what to think about particular issues. Secondly, that the wider definition of politics would mean that knowledge of central government and local government is insufficient but that the politics of everyday life would be worthy of study. Finally, that 'the ultimate test of political literacy lies in creating a proclivity to action, not in achieving more theoretical analysis' (Crick and Lister, 1978, p. 41).

This outline of Crick's ideas from the 1970s is important for putting into context the current version of political literacy. The Crick report noted that:

The term 'public life' is used in its broadest sense to encompass realistic knowledge of and preparation for conflict resolution and decision-making related to the main economic and social problems of the day, including each individual's expectations of and preparation for the world of employment, and discussion of the allocation of public resources and the rationale of taxation. Such preparations are needed whether these occur in locally, nationally or internationally concerned organisations or at any level of society from formal political institutions to informal groups, both at local or national level. (QCA/DfEE, 1998, p. 13)

In this characterisation of 'political literacy' students need to learn how to engage and participate in public life, not just learn *about* it. In a well known off-the-cuff remark reportedly made by Crick, constitutional structures are to politics what biology is to sex. It is not hard to imagine which students would prefer to learn.

It is with the above points in mind that our current project team took the decision to focus on explaining, tolerating and participating as a means of allowing young people to think and act as citizens. These three areas are, we suggest, examples of something that is fundamental about citizenship. They can be described as procedural concepts and their nature will be explored in the next section of this chapter.

## Characterising Procedural Concepts

Procedural (or second order) concepts are distinct from substantive concepts (such as government or war) that relate more narrowly to the study of particular issues. We want to help teachers to go beyond asking students to memorise details of specific cases, and also to go further than to have students consider the nature of the contexts and substantive concepts which may relate to a number of cases. The ambitious position would be to assert that by identifying procedural concepts it would be possible to invite students not just to think *about* citizenship but to think *as* citizens. Teachers and others, we hope, would be encouraged, when using procedural concepts, to move away from citizenship as 'merely' a goal and allow for the possibility of a clearer identification of what students need to do and how they should think in order to demonstrate effective learning. The curriculum materials we want to produce should relate directly to the procedural concepts that we have identified through consultation with teachers and experts.

This should not be too ambitious an aim. Similar work has already taken place in other subjects. Our understanding of educational goals for students of history, for example, has been vastly improved by the clearer identification of what is needed for pupils to think as historians. Some of this work has been influential in our own discussions. We were, for example, attracted by the following statement from Lee and Ashby (2000):

> Teaching that systematically builds on prior understandings and assessment that rewards their development are both central to achieving progression. Of course, algorithmic approaches are possible in many forms of teaching and experience in the United Kingdom unsurprisingly suggests that they are likely to be widespread where teachers do not themselves have a good grasp of the ideas they are attempting to teach. This may be the case even when entry standards are high (a first or upper second class in a degree). (p. 215)

Although the specific content and context of what is to be studied must always be emphasised, we are struck by the fact that it has now been possible in history to produce more valuable educational work by identifying the procedural concepts that characterise the field. This means that students know what they have to learn and also allows them to focus on the levels of understanding that can and should be reached in relation to each concept. Students can now focus their attention not just on learning information (e.g. names and dates), studying contexts (e.g. the 19th century) or learning about substantive concepts that are often tied to particular events (e.g. revolution). Rather, history teachers can concentrate on improving students' understanding through a clearer appreciation of such procedural concepts as evidence, cause and change. These procedural concepts can be seen as the essential part of 'doing' the subject. A shift is made in that area from learning history to being a historian. The concepts can then be developed to show levels of performance which allow for more effective and precisely targeted teaching approaches. We now know, for example, that when we look at children's conceptions of rational understanding in history, their thinking tends to conform to a pattern. Once something about these patterns is known, it may be easier to understand what pupils are thinking, and then help them develop their thinking by more precisely formulated approaches to teaching. This combination of the knowledge of the procedural concepts and knowledge of pupils' thinking may be a potent force for improvement (Lee, Dickinson and Ashby, 1994). This approach thus seeks to develop a way of knowing rather than presenting pupils with things to know. It is an approach which is seen as being 'suited to the education of citizens in a liberal democracy' as it helps students 'to develop the ability and the disposition to arrive at reasonable informed opinions' (Seixas, 2000). It is more about understanding the processes of citizenship and being citizens than about learning things about citizenship.

## Procedural Concepts and the Citizenship Education Project

It is now necessary to specify in more detail the procedural concepts that have been selected for our citizenship education project and to explain something about the practical preparations we are making for the final production of teaching and learning materials. Given that the preference is for active engagement, the expression of our procedural concepts is given in the form of active verbs. The three areas are: explaining, tolerating and participating. Expressed slightly more fully these areas would involve developing understanding dispositions and abilities associated with:

- rationality grounded in a critical appreciation of social and political realities;

- toleration within the context of a pluralistic democracy; and

- participation arising from an acceptance of one's social and political responsibilities and appreciation of one's own rights and entitlements.

These concepts have been selected following a careful considera- tion of the nature of the Citizenship Order for the curriculum and a review of the literature and discussion with experts (academics and teachers). It is, however, a provisional list and it is hoped that it will be modified during the project. It is, of course, necessary to relate the concepts to substantive concepts of citizenship, otherwise it would be possible for school students to explain and tolerate and participate in any lesson or activity in the school or community. Having asserted that there is something essential for citizenship education wrapped up in these procedural concepts, we need to be able to explain how they relate generally to an overarching sense of citizenship and how they, themselves, can be seen as being made up of necessary features. Consequently, our materials will be based around a key concept such as inequality or justice or identity. The materials and activities will be designed to encourage students:

- to explain their views, their understandings and their arguments;

- to tolerate, accommodate and reflect upon opinions and views that may be different from their own; and

- to participate in the consideration and debate of these ideas in the classroom and (ideally) use this experience and understanding in their life outside school.

It would not be possible in this chapter to give a full account of all the various aspects contained within the project. Therefore we discuss below one of the three main areas of our work, that which is related to participation.

## Participation

Citizenship is centrally about participation. If we do not consider citizenship as practised then we will be reduced to an exploration, probably in academic terms, of the meaning of legal rights and duties or encouraging a pleasant but uncritical collaboration.

There are a number of issues that need to be considered before we can be sure that participation is occurring in a way that is meaningful and appropriate for citizenship education. We must beware of not simply becoming involved in a drive to increase voter turnout. There are legitimate worries following the very low turn out in the 2001 general election that young people are becoming alienated from mainstream politics. However, there is no evidence at the moment of a generational decline in voting turnout. In other words, young people may simply grow into voting. At the age of 20 voting, like gardening, is a turn off; by the age of 50 (to paraphrase Voltaire) people are concerned with the cultivation of their gardens *and* with the new leisure activity of voting. The decision not to vote may be taken after a serious consideration of the policies offered by a range of political parties. A decision to stay at home and not vote may be a better example of participation than the exercise of a simple cross on a ballot paper every four or five years.

Young people, as shown in a number of recent research projects, are bored not by politics but by politicians. Single interest issues such as the environment, gender and law and order often excite a good deal of interest and activity. Amnesty International groups that flourish in schools are a testimony to that. Further, we cannot be content with an encouragement of activity without exploring the meaning of that encouragement. If to use the American phrase that seems to be rapidly adopted in the UK, 'service learning' is the acceptable expression of community involvement, then we would certainly hope that its purpose is acceptable. We do not necessarily want to allow private businesses to become so active that it is necessary for altruistic young people to have to bandage the wounds of the welfare state.

In any consideration of the meaning of participation there are a number of levels and contexts that can be best expressed in the form of a series of continua. The three 'levels' that are shown below would themselves need to be interpreted carefully. It would be very unhelpful if the **context** and **purpose** of participation were not con-sidered. The level of difficulty associated with each area shown below can be altered depending upon a variety of factors. We would not, for example, wish to suggest that any sort of involvement in out-of-school activities was automatically at a higher level than any sort of participation within school. For practical reasons, school students can operate only periodically at the community involve-ment end of the scale. The areas that are shown below should not be seen as if they should be ordered in a simple hierarchy. It was a deliberate decision not to number the continua shown below from

1 to 4. Rather, it may be more useful to see them as elements that can be used to understand the sort of participation that is occurring with the final area (participating – engaging), allowing us to think about the type of activity that is going on in the other three areas.

## Active thinking, physical activity

Pupils do not need to move around a classroom in order to participate. Participation may be achieved by some careful individual thinking – although many teachers would hope that this would generate some kind of action or involvement by the pupil. We need to bear in mind the distinction between encouraging pupils to explain about participation and actually participating.

## Individually generated activity, working with, or in relation to, others

It is important to emphasise that great sophistication may be achieved by individuals. The nature of leadership is clearly an example of effective participation. However, there are differences between those who would be able to participate in an activity in the 'backroom' (speech writing, creating posters etc) and those who can work effectively with others. The activities of those who are operating at higher levels might be more explicitly to do with, for example, support mobilisation through making effective presentations.

## Participation in school, participation in other contexts

It is useful to consider the range of contexts within which pupils can participate. Some pupils will have more opportunities to participate outside school; others will, for a range of reasons, find it easier to become involved in events at school. Perhaps the key consideration is to reflect on the possibility that pupils will need to be able to operate in different locations, transferring learning from one context to another.

## Participating, engaging

It may be possible to make a distinction between merely taking part in and getting 'under the skin' of issues. This should not lead to an insistence upon particular mind-sets of learners. Rather, there should be a sense in which the issues mean something to the learners. They are able to participate not because they have been told to, but because they can see the value of becoming involved. This allows for the avoidance of simply saying that the pupils took part in a role-play, so they must be able to participate effectively.

The above issues lead to complex challenges. Certainly we do not claim to provide simple and straightforward answers to these matters by providing classroom resources. However, we do suggest that classroom resources can be given a focus arising from our aims and that a discussion of the teaching and learning that takes place may help us to clarify the issues still further. The following can be given as examples from the learning resources we are producing:

- a debate in a history lesson recreating a public meeting involving suffragettes, members of parliament, women who were not suffragettes and factory owners. The exercise is pre- ceded by a task to help students explain the circumstances. Role cards are distributed and then students are asked to under- take research and complete a preparation sheet. The debate is structured with the teacher or a student acting as chair.

- Discussion of an extract from James Joyce's *Portrait of the Artist as a Young Man* in which a school student is beaten, is followed by 'freeze frame action'. The students present three freeze frames and give their sequence a one-word title. Certain members of each group are 'hot seated' so they can elaborate upon their character's actions. The scenes are then replayed with opportunities for stopping the action and developing a different conclusion. Students are asked to reflect upon the nature of their own participation in relation to objectives relevant to citizenship.

- A story of a boy or girl working for low wages in difficult conditions on the production of sports kits or footballs. Following work on explanation and the acceptability of such incidents, students are asked to consider a list of action statements that are designed to promote better understanding of possible routes to action.

## Challenges

It would not be realistic if we were to pretend that the above approach could be developed in a simple and straightforward manner. We attempt to draw attention in this section of the chapter to a range of obstacles and we feel sure that other issues will emerge as the trialling of our materials proceeds.

Some of these critical issues are fundamental. From the policy makers' perspective it is interesting that Marshall's work on citizenship, that is now seen as being so influential, does not figure in any of the references used when political literacy was making an impression in the 1970s. Marshall did explore the growth and meaning of political rights and showed how this could be helpfully used in a characterisation of citizenship. But apart from the general criticisms about the validity of Marshall's ideas (see Heater, 1999) we need also to ask if the use of a wider definition of politics still allows for a separate strand of political literacy in a framework for citizenship. If social and moral responsibility and community involvement are themselves examples of a broader understanding of the political, then the internal coherence of political literacy as an integrated but perhaps also discrete part of citizenship may raise more questions than it answers. Indeed the rather worrying omission of the term 'political literacy' from the *National Curriculum Orders for Citizenship* (QCA/DfEE, 1999) suggests that careful observation and hard work is needed if negative possibilities are to be avoided (Davies, 1999).

We should be aware that there is a possibility that teachers' thinking on citizenship does at times tend to avoid political matters (Davies, Gregory and Riley, 1999). It is extremely important to note Pring's

(1999) characterisation of attempts at political education which have tended to ignore genuinely political initiatives precisely because they were seen as oppositional and dangerous. Pring senses that the whole approach to classifying tightly defined learning outcomes is itself an illustration of a political approach that will direct and manage learning but will not allow learners to develop genuine political understanding or become involved in real political issues. Although his analysis suffers from something of a reality gap in its approach to the current means of educational reform, his views do carry something of a warning for all those who want to promote political literacy.

Perhaps the central difficulty for teachers is the relationship between their work and the wider political context. The factors that led to a demand for political education in the 1970s generally allowed for at least the possibility of good work. The lowering of the age of majority to 18, research that showed high levels of political ignorance among the young, the realisation that textbooks were full of political messages that young people could not learn from, even implicitly, resulted in a more professional and worthwhile approach. However, as has been noted above, the context in the early 1990s was far less benign and led to less valuable discussions about education. It is always important to ask – and difficult to know – what sort of context we are currently experiencing.

More pragmatically, we need to raise questions about the vehicles through which citizenship education will develop. For the purposes of this project the following have been established:

- a personal and social education team that has created lessons around citizenship issues that emerge from sport;

- a history team whose members have focused their efforts on women's rights in the past, the present and the future; and

- an English team that has concentrated on justice in local communities.

Each of these teams is made up of practising teachers. For the purposes of the project they operated for the most part in pairs. It was felt that they would have more force or presence in their own schools if they were not speaking as lone individuals. These teams also included at least one member of the project that was based either at a university or in a non-governmental organisation for the purposes of adding experience and expertise to the production of curriculum materials that can be used across a number of different schools. We have shared readings (e.g. Kerr, 2000; Morton, no date; Lee, Dickinson and Ashby, 1994; Newmann and Wehlage, 1993) and then held discussions in the form almost of a readers' circle. We chose to work in these three 'subject' areas for particular reasons. But still doubts may remain about whether we can achieve appropriate and effective change.

Personal and Social Education (PSE) may well become *the* area of the school that is regarded as the principal home of citizenship education. There are clearly a number of advantages to this: there are many skilled teachers already in place; it has timetable space; there is a clear overlap between citizenship education and the sorts of issues that PSE teachers have been concerned with for a long time; there are networks of people and associations that are already in place and which may be able to facilitate the difficult challenge of implementation. Of course, we should also be a little wary about the potential of PSE. At times it has rather emphasised the personal over the political. It has not enjoyed high status in some schools. It lacks key features of the apparatus of a 'normal' school subject (such as examinations) and while there are advantages to this there may also be certain disadvantages. In some schools PSE has been organised or managed by a specialist who has been recruited from another area of the school and then largely staffed by people who are filling up spaces on a 'proper' timetable. Above all, PSE may itself carry so many debates and issues that the addition of citizenship will bring further fragmentation rather than greater coherence.

History also has a series of advantages and disadvantages. Well known political scientists (such as Bernard Crick) have referred to the importance of history for understanding contemporary society. Without the root of history, politics can bear no fruit. History is the way in which we understand questions of identity and a springboard that helps us determine what we might become. It cannot predict the future but it can help us to think about it more meaningfully. History deals with those matters that are central to a democratic society. Once we have the opportunity to think, for example, about the meaning of a multicultural society it may be easier for us to be able to tackle contemporary issues. It also develops a range of skills that are highly relevant. Students will, as a matter of course, be encouraged to analyse sources, exercise judgement, and learn to make a reasoned argument. And these students undertake this work in a way that is always relatively 'safe'. The tensions and sensitivities associated with contemporary events at times get in the way of educational work. History provides a training ground or a form of role play in which we can learn to think and respond by seeing what others did. The need to place oneself in the shoes of others is an excellent opportunity to practise understanding in more than a cognitive sense. It is perhaps a training ground for toleration.

English similarly provides excellent opportunities for relevant work. Much English literature is an illustration and an illumination of the nature of society. Many examples can be given. *Nineteen Eighty-Four, To Kill a Mockingbird, Brave New World, The Colour Purple, Northern Lights, Skellig* are just a few examples of adult and contemporary children's fiction which tell us about our feelings (social and moral responsibility), our relationships with others (community involvement) and the nature of power (political literacy). In order to express these feelings and ideas we need to be skilled users of the English language. We need to ask school students to come to understand the text by considering simple comprehension as well as the motive of the author in the form of intended impact. We also want to encourage students to be able to make a presentation themselves. To craft a response (orally or in writing) that is appropriate for a particular audience, they have to be clear about what they want to say and be able to say (or write) it in a way that makes sense.

Subjects like history and English may have to overcome difficult challenges if they are to educate successfully for citizenship. Teachers of these subjects often justify their work in terms of the relevance to contemporary society. But, in fact, they are really academic specialists who have entered teaching so as to pursue their love of the 19th century or the novels of Jane Austen. There would be nothing wrong with this (some of our best teachers are good academic specialists). But there are interesting issues to consider. Are teachers really interested in citizenship? Even if the teachers are interested, do the pupils know that they are interested? If teachers and pupils are both in agreement that they are involved in education for citizenship then are we sure about the best way in which appropriate goals are achieved? For some teachers the best way to develop citizenship education might be to promote the capacity for rational thought. This ability could be exercised in the future in a range of contexts in contemporary society. Others will suggest that rational thought in itself is not enough, that there must be a determination to explore key citizenship topics, and to do so in a way that means that opportunities to practise effective citizenship are available.

When discussing these issues it is most important to encourage teachers to specify the real nature of their work. In all the above contexts (PSE, English, History) teachers may be able to develop a line of reasoning that initially sounds persuasive but which on closer examination appears rather unacceptable. For example, a history teacher may suggest that it is important to consider the use of power to improve public welfare. This is a citizenship issue. But what if the pupils spend a lesson learning some information about the design of Roman aqueducts and are asked to draw their own pictures of these structures? Surely this is not necessarily good history, let alone citizenship education. There are particular challenges that history teachers have to face if they are to persuade colleagues and students that political literacy can be worthwhile. Heater (1974) has written about the potential of history teaching for political literacy but he has also (1978) outlined a number of potential difficulties. Political literacy is essentially concerned with enabling the individual to operate in contemporary society whereas history 'can provide only perspective and comparison – no mean contribution but nevertheless not the totality' (p. 116). The topics that are taught in history lessons did not engage the interest of the majority of the population or, still less, offer even at the time opportunities for involvement. On similar lines, what would we think if a PSE teacher explained that a good way to develop community involvement would be for a Christmas party to be organised? With no opportunities for reflection about critical social issues, the nature of who has taken the decision to follow through on this task and the use of particular pupils in specific roles, this is a pleasant but potentially vacuous enterprise. Perhaps an English teacher might suggest looking at the character of *Jude the Obscure*, claiming that it illustrates issues about social exclusion. If, in practice, the students fail to see the novel in terms of the teacher's aims, they may read the book 'merely' as the story of a tormented person who experiences gross bad luck, or as an example of a particular literary style. If so, then it will remain an English lesson and not really be about anything else. Clearly the relationship between subjects like history and English and citizenship education needs to be considered carefully. The possibility of using citizenship education to improve the way in which subjects like history and English are taught raises a range of interesting possibilities. J. F. Kennedy once exhorted people not to ask what their country could do for them, but rather to ask what they could do for their country. 'Mainstream' subject specialists and 'newly arrived' teachers of citizenship need to reflect on what they can do for each other.

## Conclusion

We are working positively in an attempt to provide some useful practical ways forward. We want to provide examples of what can be done in classrooms but also hope to encourage further debate about what essentially counts in citizenship education. The arguments and debates will not be brought to a swift conclusion. Indeed it would be most unhelpful if it suddenly were imagined that someone had managed to find the essence of citizenship. We certainly hope for ongoing debates. But we hope also to narrow the current range of discussion so that we have a practical focus that allows for professional development. In the next few years in England there will be a wonderful opportunity for lively debates and some vitally important educational work.

# 4

# Ethnocentric narratives and the 'European dimension' in historical education

Aristotle A. Kallis

We have all been told, at many stages in our education, that history has two educational functions. Firstly, it is an essential constituent element in the construction of individual or group identity – be this national, regional (on the importance of the 'regional' dimension in education see Montané, 1995), local or any combination thereof. This function is achieved through the systematic articulation of the past in a way that fosters ideas of belonging, pride in the historical trajectory of a people and admiration at its most honourable enterprises. Secondly, it is widely assumed that a knowledge of the past encourages a deeper understanding of the historical forces that have been responsible for failures and calamities. In this sense history holds the key to a constructive dialectical relation between memory, present experience and future expectations. Thus historical education constitutes both an integral element of the process of 'making' citizens and a projection of the Enlightenment belief that knowledge and rational analysis can improve the human condition and contribute to the attainment of universally superior goals.

The teaching of history has acquired a central position in national (and increasingly sub-national, that is regional, local and minority) curricula. The intellectual validity of such an educational choice is rarely questioned: for the last two centuries the predominant experience of *belonging* to a community has been based on a belief in national or ethnic community. In most cases such a community is politically identified with a current state structure, thus attaching the individual to the cultural, political and historic attributes of the national state. Such an imaginary link has proved to be emotionally powerful, prevailing over alternative projects of cultivating trans-national loyalties: firstly socialism, and more recently cosmo-politanism and multiculturalism, have failed in the majority of cases to mitigate the emotional cogency of nationalism, nor have they questioned the primacy of ethnicity as the defining constituent element of personal and group identity. History and national identity have been far more linked in a dialectical (as opposed to a linear) way: the narratives of *national* history – which in theory present an 'objective' re-construction of the past derived from the alleged continuity of the national community through the centuries – actually become potent devices for producing and fostering a sense of national wholeness through a re-ordering of a pool of past events that is fundamentally 'subjective'. In other words, the re-constructed historic narratives of the past both reflect and advance identification with the national community. This identifi-cation is more 'imaginary' or 'invented' than objective (see for example, Anderson, 1991; or Gellner, 1983); but history serves the crucial purpose of infusing a sort of empirical validity to this other-wise subjective enterprise. In fact, in many cases it has become a pivotal aspect of the re-nationalisation of the masses, both in the West (with the rise of the civic neo-nationalisms) and in the East (with the violent recurrence of post-socialist ethno-religious dis-courses). Along with language, religion, geography and folklore, history has always been a crucial determinant of belonging.

The project of European integration, and its current concern with the promotion of a new sense of inclusive *European* civic identity associated with citizenship, presents a challenging task that embraces the whole rationale, organisation and delivery of historical education. The meeting of the EC Council and the Ministers for Education on the 'European dimension' in education ratified Resolution 88/C/177/02 on the 24 May 1988. The aim was to reinforce a European perspective of education with the support of the Member States and the trans-national European institutions in relation to initiatives in a number of fields: this included education policy, curricula, preparation of teaching material, teacher training and the promotion of exchanges between pupils and teachers in the various Member States.[1] For historical education, the challenge lay in how the past might be re-articulated so that the understandable emphasis on national particularism could at the same time accommodate and foster the novel idea of trans-national loyalty and belonging to a wider cultural, political and historic entity of Europe.

This chapter presents a case-study of the teaching of the history of the Second World War – with its polarising and emotionally charged entanglements – as an example of how different educational curricula treat a recent, 'uncomfortable' European historical experience; and how the current treatment may be modified to respond constructively to the changes that the discourse on 'European identity' has either effected or wishes to promote.

As with every other military conflict the 1939–1945 war offers opportunities to extol *national* traits, to articulate a Manichean vision of recent history, to provide blanket justifications for political choices and to minimise or eliminate critical assessments of inopportune national aspirations. The exceptionalism of this particular conflict lies in its still strong emotive residual power in collective memory and in its capacity to re-articulate a deeply divisive image of European history as the aggregate of the antagonistic and unstable interaction between nation-states. I will argue that – in spite of the positive developments that enable more dispassionate narratives and increased pluralism in interpretation – the teaching of Second World War history remains largely entrenched in the rationale of ethnocentricity. The chapter highlights some major shortcomings of current narratives and examines procedures and strategies that may allow historical education within the context of a *European* educational dimension to make a more constructive contribution to the promotion of European citizenship. The crucial task that faces both historians and educationalists is to establish a more constructive framework of interaction: on the national/regional/local level, in the sense of a better relation between academic research and educational curricula; and on the 'European' level, through the extension of co-operation between academics and educationalists across the European countries and regions with a view to promoting more plural, multi-layered and open narratives. This underlines that the quality of textbooks is but one of many issues associated with the nature of historical education. If the fundamental shortcomings of historical education have to be addressed in the extension of a civic European identity, then the task of recasting and enriching narratives cannot be performed by either educationalists alone or exclusively within the boundaries of every state.

## Teaching the Second World War: toward a more pluralistic educational framework

It is acknowledged that exploring twentieth-century history solely from the viewpoint of the nation-state is an unintelligible project that misconstrues narratives and interpretations. In teaching the Second World War in its full complexity – both as a short-term conflict and as the culmination of longer-term trends in European history such as the second 'Thirty Years War' that started in 1914 and ended with the traumatic events of 1945 – the need to combine national and international perspectives has been acknowledged and reflected in recent changes in two key areas of the history textbooks: impartiality and scope of coverage.

### Impartiality

With the collapse of interwar fascism and the cessation of the hostilities in 1945 the task of reconstructing Europe out of the ruins of the Second World War embraced both material and intellectual considerations. Although the conventional notion that writing history requires a chronological and emotional distance from the events inhibited an immediate reassessment of the 1939–45 period, the unprecedented brutality and destruction that were unleashed during the Second World War haunted every national historical narrative. The task of finding suitable explanations for these events initially fell to academic research. The experience of six years of horrifying violence – coupled with the shocking balance sheet of the war in terms of human and material destruction – inevitably placed a moral burden on the historical interpretations of the pre-1939 period. Initially, the main problem was how to 'historicise' the deviation of interwar societies from the Enlightenment model of rationality, tolerance and freedom; in other words, how far could these extreme conditions be linked to previous intellectual and social developments in European history. The first response of the historical profession was to treat this ruthless deviation as emanating from the 'demonic' personalities of specific interwar leaders and a narrow group of followers. However, given that charismatic leaders cannot alone account for the popularity of extreme ideas such as fascism across the continent, the idea that Europe was suffering from a 'moral disease' was also put forward (for a discussion of this, see Hagtvet and Kuhnl, 1980). Both these interpretations betrayed an attempt to treat the interwar period in terms of an exceptional (and short-lived) divergence from an orthodox path, which European history re-joined in 1945. This was a strangely mollifying narrative, that assumed that the norm of the European historic trajectory was alien to the forces unleashed in the 1919–1945 period. But this conclusion was predicated on rejecting the notion that this 'uncomfortable' past could be historicised in its potential long-term relevance to the European cognitive model.

The 1951 educational agreement between France and Germany was the first step towards producing a more pluralistic and versatile framework for the teaching of the 1870–1933 period in the two countries. This bilateral initiative came only a few years after the French government had introduced an imaginative student exchange programme between France and the French-occupied zone in Germany (cf. Mazower, 1999). With the failure and eventual abandonment of the 'de-nazification' project (primarily pursued by the American authorities) the emphasis shifted to establishing a new framework of cultural co-operation and ending the historical fault-line that had divided Germany from its Western allies since the beginning of the twentieth century. The 1951 educational agreement came at a sensitive time in the re-organisation of both countries; but immediate progress was made in the content, presentation and quality of textbooks in the two history curricula. For example, the previous French curriculum had exonerated the Versailles Treaty, while the German equivalent had ferociously castigated this. Both gave way to a more dispassionate and multi-layered interpretation that combined hindsight with at least an acknowledgement of the existence of parallel perspectives and historic perceptions on this sensitive issue.

The real breakthrough came in the 1960s and 1970s, in a more favourable political conjuncture for the radical reassessment of educational practices. New and bolder academic research had questioned the main assumptions of the immediate post-war excision of fascism from the body of the European intellectual development. It is not surprising that this trend was pioneered in Germany itself. With the ground-breaking publications of Fritz Fischer in the 1960s the notion that National Socialism was a culmination of long-term trends in modern German history since unification questioned the conventional portrayal of nazism as a historic aberration (Fischer, 1967; Weidenfeld and Nicolson 1975). Predictably, such an irreverent revision provoked furious reactions from more nationalist-minded sectors of public opinion and from the academic community; but by the 1970s, Fischer's views had made their way into mainstream historical knowledge and education.

Similar painful reassessments took place in France after the withdrawal of General De Gaulle from French politics. The strength of the Gaullist post-war myths (*resistance*, the Vichy 'non-state', fascism and anti-Semitism as an 'alien import' in France) started to subside in the 1970s and particularly the 1980s, and a new political and cultural environment was much more receptive to a reassessment of French historical narratives (cf. Frey, 1999, 205–16 and 239–51). International academic scholarship in the early 1970s – for example, Robert Paxton's groundbreaking account of Vichy France (Paxton, 2001) – raised painful questions about continuities in twentieth-century French history that were a challenge to the Gaullist orthodoxy of the Vichy 'parenthesis'. Although these debates initially took place outside the confines of the French historical community, their revisionist potential made an impact on indigenous debates that unfolded in the 1980s, in a typically dynamic but also acrimonious fashion (for example, the 'Sternhell controversy', especially after the 1986 publication). Since then, a series of traditionally taboo issues – the popular roots of anti-Semitism in France, the collaborationist activities during the period of German occupation, and even the responsibility of French states-men for alienating German public opinion both in 1919 and in 1923 (with the violent occupation of the Ruhr) – have been more openly deliberated.

In Italy the process of coming to terms with the Fascist experience has been conspicuously slower and more agonising than in Germany. The country's expansionist aspirations in the First World War (irredentism, colonialism) remain largely impervious to critical assessment. However, the re-founding of the Italian state in 1946 as a republic produced a historical gap between pre-war and post-war national history. This in turn encouraged a more dispassionate view of the misguided Italian nationalism in the first half of the 20th century and de-legitimised traditional aspirations in Africa and the Mediterranean. As in Germany, the failure of the Italian bourgeoisie to come out decisively in favour of a modern democratic and pacifist agenda, as well as its failure to react to the rise and radicali-sation of fascism, are admissions that have gradually gained ground in mainstream national historical narratives. But the conservative retrenchment that characterised the Italian political environment in the 1970s and 1980s attempted to re-direct the process of revising the traditional historical narratives of the First Italian Republic in a direction that questioned the orthodox distinction between Fascism and resistance (*Resistenza*) as the moral foundation for the estab-lishment of the post-1946 Italian state (see, for example, Ledeen, 1979). Similar projects came to the fore in France and, in particular, Germany, especially with the *Historikerstreit* (see the collection of articles from the *Historikerstreit* in *Forever in the shadow of Hitler*, 1993) but, unlike Italy, they failed to command the majority political and academic view. But in Italy, attempts to present Italian fascism as more benign and modernising than National Socialism found a significantly more receptive socio-political milieu and pro-vided a fundamentally different basis for re-aligning historical revision. This said, although the serious reassessment of the country's role in the First World War, of the parameters of the *Resistenza* and of the 'anti-Fascist' moral foundation of the Italian Republic has taken place at a relatively slower pace (given the significance of such narratives in the whole post-war break with the Fascist legacy), it has acquired a new momentum in the last decade, producing more nuanced and layered historical accounts of the country's recent history, that has been reflected in the quality of recent history textbooks for secondary education.

In Greece, three traditionally taboo issues have recently made a rather modest appearance in school history textbooks: the quasi-fascist nature of the Metaxas dictatorship of 1936–41; the ideo-logical divisions and antagonisms in the national resistance against occupation by the Axis powers; and the 1945–49 civil war between communist ex-resistance organisations and the reconstituted Greek army. It should be noted that left-wing resistance movements were not recognised by the Greek state and not mentioned in textbooks until the early 1980s, except in relation to the civil war (pejoratively described as 'gang war'). However, the opening of the debate in the last two decades, the rhetoric of national reconciliation and the demise of the Cold War have favoured the discussion of Greek opposition to the Nazis, and thus provided a more elaborate under-standing of the acrimonious civil war period.

## Scope of coverage

A second area in which there has been a notable improvement in the history curricula is in the chronological and geographical coverage of historical developments and processes. The traditional view of historical education – a framework of re-ordering the past to produce a linear *national* narrative with a rigid continuity linking the fragments of the past to the present – tended to provide an insular view of historical causality within only a national framework. This view has begun slowly to give way to historical accounts that recognise the impact of international forces and developments, and the interaction between the historical experiences of a large array of countries. Although the various curricula have largely maintained the emphasis on national – as opposed to a 'European' or 'global' – history, they have made conscious efforts to expand the inclusion of material relating to the experiences of other countries/regions/ continents and to integrate national experience into a wider framework of international historical change. Recent textbooks have successfully combined the conventional narratives of linear national history with wider developments in European and world history, such as the Versailles Treaty, the dialectics of democracy and dictatorship in the 1920s and 1930s, the impact of global economic depression, the influence of communism outside the Soviet Union and the cultural climate of the interwar period. This allows the account of domestic developments to maintain its focus on national particularism and thus fulfil the function of cultivating a sense of historical national identity amongst the students. At the same time the new narratives serve to remind them that national history does not unfold in a vacuum or in a linear pattern determined only by indigenous trends.

This multi-layered framework of analysis, combining 'particular' and 'general' (that is, European and global) perspectives, encourages attempts to provide comparative narratives and a wider coverage of other countries' experiences and viewpoints. This is of particular significance for 'ambiguous' historical events and decisions that affected countries differently, and have consequently been assessed by them in divergent ways. Traditional ethnocentric narratives are not inclined to promote comparative analysis or awareness of how historical data might be appraised in fundamentally different – yet not necessarily inaccurate or unacceptably biased – ways. The example of the Versailles Treaty and the subsequent occupation of the Ruhr by France in 1923, in retaliation to Germany's inability to meet reparations, highlights this point clearly. While from a French point of view the treaty was a perhaps exaggerated but political necessary guarantee against German aggression (and, therefore, the violent occupation of German territory was a legally sound response to Germany's violation of one of the treaty's conditions), the discourse of 'humiliation' and 'loss of sovereignty' that underpinned interwar German nationalist responses to the *Diktat* provides an interesting psychological perspective. In a more dispassionate context of comparative historical analysis, this helps students appreciate how decisions made with a valid national rationale may impact on other countries in substantially different and unforeseen ways. Similarly, accounts of the Greek-Turkish war of 1920–22 have benefited from a dialectical examination of the two national perspectives. Students in the Greek history curriculum in the 1990s have been exposed to more dispassionate narratives, distancing their interpretation from the psychological trauma of the defeat and emphasising that what was for one side 'vindication of victory' and 'legitimate historical claim' was for the other 'unacceptable humiliation' and 'occupation'. Such combination of perspectives allows students 'to contrast developments in different countries or regions and to identify trends and patterns, similarities and differences' (cf. Stradling, 2001, 30–1).

At the same time, the weakening of the traditional assumption that history teaching should deal with events with the benefit of historical 'distance' – which had resulted in a conventional *terminus ante quem* in most historical narratives of around 1945 – has encouraged a more holistic view of twentieth-century history, linking pre- and post-World War Two periods and bringing history much closer to the experience of young people. Increasingly, the successful pursuit of security, economic co-operation and cultural/political convergence in post-war Europe are becoming legitimate loci of historical education, with an emphasis on the development of such trans-national European institutions as the EC/EU and the Council of Europe. The contrast between pre-war aggressive nationalism and conflict and post-war peaceful co-existence and joint pursuit of common goals is a powerful image to mitigate students' conventional views of European history as a litany of wars, antagonism and mutual hatred. Again, the demise of the Cold War has removed the ideological necessity to designate no-go areas in historical education. Taking Greece as an example, the turbulent post-war history of the country can now be discussed without the ideological filter of anti-communism, in sharp contrast to the state's present institutional stability and modernisation. A similar dis-passionate narrative may be seen in post-Cold War German textbooks with references to the DDR and the 'success' of the re-unification project.

There is a crucial link between this widening of the chronological coverage and the promotion of a strong 'European dimension' in historical education. On the qualitative level, the methodological exposure of the discipline of history to the methodologies and foci of the social sciences in recent decades has given historical educa-tion a stronger comparative insight and a more fruitful cognitive association between history and political science. The inclusion of the post-1945 period has contributed substantially to unifying the historical narrative of post-war European co-operation with the specific political analysis of European integration within the European Union, the Council of Europe and other similar trans-national European organisations. As mentioned earlier, this is of decisive importance in bringing young people into closer historical contact with the progress of the European project since the 1950s and in underlining recent progress in the construction of a concept of 'European citizenship'.

There is, however, an equally crucial quantitative dimension to the intensification of the European dimension of historical education. Until recently national curricula provided only cursory treatment of international and post-1945 history. The distinction between 'national' and 'international' historical courses, in conjunction with the predominant ethnocentric view of teaching history as a mechanism to develop students' nationalism, resulted in the allocation of very limited teaching time to European and global perspectives on historical change. A similar discrepancy was evident in the teaching of 'contemporary' or 'twentieth-century' history, with a disproportionate focus on pre-1945 coverage at the expense of post-WW2 developments. Given that the 'European' focus in the narratives of the first half of the century largely converged on a negative view of the European legacy (the two world wars, international competition, authoritarianism and totalitarianism), the positive European dimension of the post-1945 period was generally reduced to an atrophied supplement. There have been signs of change in this direction in the last two decades. In most countries the balance between the pre- and post-1945 periods has been revised to allow a more detailed treatment of contemporary developments. There has been a similar significant increase in the time allocated to the teaching of modern/contemporary history (in comparison to ancient, medieval or early-modern history) (Pinkel, 2000). This has enabled a more in-depth treatment of contemporary historical developments – and of European co-operation – with a stronger emphasis on the positive dimensions of this, providing an effective link between national and European (and even global) experience.

## Persisting flaws: the legacy of ethnocentricity

In spite of these positive developments the rationale and structure of historical education still have a strong residue of ethnocentricity, largely unresponsive to the emergence of new parallel loyalties and limited by the model of 'nation-state' history. I am not suggesting that the nation-state has become significantly less relevant to the production of individual identities. There is still, however, a relatively slow response to demonstrate that *post-war European co-operation is the result of, not the cause of, a sense of historic and cultural affinity* amongst European peoples and states. This new reality underscores how important it is to re-articulate European and national history in a way that makes a constructive contribution to the discourse of European identity and citizenship.

## 'Redeeming the nation'

The first stumbling block relates to the choice of foci for the national curricula. However open-minded the presentation of national history has become in recent textbooks, there is still a hard core of national values and choices that are judged to be worth defending, justifying or accenting. German textbooks allocate much space to the resistance to Hitler, either by popular movements to Hitler and Nazism, or by prominent figures – for example, the July 1944 plot against Hitler, or the opposition to the invasion of Czechoslovakia in 1938–39 by conservative officers). In Italy, challenging the post-war anti-Fascist orthodoxy has proved a formidable enterprise. The accentuation of the role of the *Resistenza* and of the exiled dissidents has been dominant, while there is reluctance to critically assess the country's aspirations in the First World War as a prelude to the interwar expansionist discourse in Italy. The result attempts to salvage the *Risorgimento* imagery and the 'just' aspirations of Italian nationalism from the blanket castigation of Fascism as a historic anomaly in the course of national history. There is also a disproportionate emphasis on Italy's contribution to the war *after* the collapse of the Fascist regime in 1943. In Greece, textbooks generally reproduce the irredentist discourse of 'unredeemed' lands (by opting for the term 'northern Epirus' to designate those territories of the Albanian state inhabited by a Greek-speaking minority; or by referring to the question of Cyprus as a central issue of national interest). The advances of Greek armed forces into Albanian territory are conceptualised as 'liberation'. The narrative concentrates heavily on the victorious stages of the war, on the jubilant response of Greek public opinion to victories and on the 'heroic' defeat by the 'vastly superior' German forces.

### 'Extolling the nation'

Since the strength of national identity emanates from pride and a strong sense of achievement, it is understandable that the teaching of the Second World War carefully elaborates on the individual positive contributions of each country. A common feature of most textbooks is the reference to their participation in joint military operations (for example, French resistance in the invasion of Sicily and the landing in Normandy; the participation of the Greek army and navy in the operations in north Africa). In addition, every textbook provides ample evidence of national triumph and perseverance. German textbooks stress the issue of the devastation of German cities from the largely punitive Allied bombings, especially towards the end of the war. The endurance of the British population during the period of the *Luftwaffe* bombardments of 1941, linked to the notion that 'Britain alone' sustained the war against the Axis after the Nazi victories in continental Europe, are given extensive coverage in British textbooks. Greek textbooks, on the other hand, extol the defence of national territory against Italian aggression, stress the theme of the 'first victory against the Axis' and praise the delaying of the German advance in the Balkans as an indirect contribution to the failure of Operation Barbarossa against the Soviet Union. An interesting angle in the narrative is the link made between the 'heroic' defeat in *Thermopylae* in 1941 and the sacrifice of the ancient Spartan forces at the same location in the context of the Greek-Persian wars of the fifth century BC. This association carefully invokes the imagery of a glorious ancient past, fostering the idea of continuity in Greek culture and presenting the preservation of Greece as the result of a diachronic display of heroism and sacrifice by the Greek people.

### National 'specificity' and the 'other'

Notwithstanding the attempts to re-proportion the emphasis on national history, the predominantly ethnocentric approach under-pins the structure, periodisation and interpretive framework of teaching modern European history. An example is offered by the conventional treatment of Italian Fascism in the country's textbooks. Extending the academic debate in Italy about the nature of Fascism and its alleged similarities to Nazism, attempts were made to concentrate on the dissimilarities between Mussolini's regime and Hitler's Germany: the former's lack of a totalitarian structure, the relative restraint in the use of terror, the half-hearted endorsement of anti-Semitism, the regime's flirtation with modernity, and its political enslavement to Hitler's aggressive agenda. The rationale of this enterprise is, of course, not to do with mitigating the overwhelmingly critical official view of Mussolini and the Fascist regime: the point is to link the regime's failure to emulate the more radical and destructive aspects of Nazism to long-term trends in Italian history and psyche. Fascism is thus presented as an overall negation of the post-unification traditions of Italy: the roots of liberalism, the individualism of the Italian people, their cultural ideals and instinctive aversion to imposed holistic projects. Particular emphasis is placed on the more lenient treatment of the Jewish population by the Italian occupying forces – although some limited references to the policies of racial discrimination policies in Ethiopia and Libya have eventually made their appearance in text-books.

Another example is offered by the attitude towards the Metaxas dictatorship in the Greek textbooks: not only is there an obvious endeavour to trivialise the fascist aspects of the regime and to emphasise its 'realism' (as opposed to the ideological fanaticism of its German and Italian counterparts); but also Metaxas himself is portrayed as a leader of good nationalist credentials who, in declaring war against Italy, expressed the heroic spirit and determination of the whole Greek people. The tendency to shift the blame for the less 'heroic' aspects of the war effort to 'others' is mani-fested in a number of occasions in the narrative. The failure of the Greek armed forces to hold back the Nazi advance in the spring of 1941 is partly attributed to the inefficiency of Yugoslav defence. By the same token, the deterioration of the internal situation in Greece after the liberation of in 1944 is increasingly associated with mistakes of the Greek government and the leadership of the communist resistance but, according to the textbook interpretation, a large portion of blame lay with the 'forces of international intervention' that manipulated the situation and influenced the Greek political establishment to extend their control over Greek affairs.

## The 'European dimension' of historical education: challenges and strategies

This brief analysis of approaches and interpretations of the Second World War in the secondary education curricula of a selection of European countries serves as a case-study for the assessment of both the progress and the persisting stumbling blocks in the way history is taught to a younger generation of people who have grown up in the reality of European integration. Generally, recent developments in revising the content, structure and delivery of history curricula in Europe have been motivated by an increasing awareness that the 'European' perspective can be effectively accommodated within, and promoted through, a constructive interaction between the national particularism and a wider 'European dimension' (cf. Beernaert, Van Dijk and Sander, 1993). Initial suspicions that 'the unique and the particular in a nation's or region's history is subsumed by the need to focus on the more generalisable patterns' have significantly subsided in the face of a growing realisation that the 'European dimension' in historical education does not require a dilution of the various national narratives in order to conform to a grand 'European scheme' (*Ibid*, 25–7). Instead, comparative methodologies promoting the 'juxtaposition of similar phenomena in different cultures' (Bloch, 1928, pp. 15–50) may be successfully employed in history curricula to maintain interest in national particularities and at the same time integrating this with a wider pattern of historical convergence in Europe, that updates historical narratives in the current process of integration and co-operation. In the end, far from being an impediment to plural loyalties or transnational allegiances, history can, and indeed should, play a more affirmative role in the promotion of a new type of identity for the new Europeans.

In this sense, one of the main educational tasks facing those responsible for the structure and delivery of historical education in European countries concerns redressing the balance between the horizontal (trans-national perspectives, comparative analysis and a broad 'European' viewpoint) and the vertical (national history in the *longue durée*, attention to national particularism) axes of historical narratives. At the moment, the legacy of the conventional emphasis on the vertical axis remains a powerful methodological model, furnishing a misleadingly linear view of national history, whose insularity – if not sometimes parochialism – inhibits a meaningful dialogue with wider European and international forces. The traditional distinction between courses on 'national' and on 'international' history raises two fundamental questions of crucial significance for the debate on strengthening the horizontal dimension in historical education. The first relates to the positioning of the 'European dimension' within this 'national-international' axis. Should the autonomy of national history be maintained, thus forcing the discussion of the European perspective into the wider global focus? Alternatively, does the European level provide history curricula with a highly effective and meaningful unifying link between the two traditional poles of the axis, thus encouraging a fundamental rethinking of the wide categories of historical education? There is no general consensus on this dilemma at the moment, although it has to be noted that the 'European dimension' has made significant inroads into the national historical narratives, sometimes in a highly effective comparative framework, but more often in a rather disjointed and largely muddled manner.

But the problem of a constructive re-organisation of national historical narratives in order to accommodate the growing significance of the European perspective brings us to the second question – is the conventional matrix of chronological accounts suitable for promoting the horizontal axis of historical education? The vertical narrative model creates – or perhaps contrives – continuities and interprets discontinuities in the essentially linear historical pattern in a manner that is unsuitable for setting national trends into a wider

European perspective. An alternative model of reconstructing the past may be a more thematic approach that is both national and inter-national – European and global – in which an emphasis on wider phenomena and trends allows a horizontal comparison of various national experiences, their interaction and their cumulative effect on the long-term trajectory of European history. This is an alternative methodology that has not as yet been explored with sufficient daring by the planners of history curricula or by the authors of history textbooks. This kind of thematic approach to national and global history can be criticised as not suited to the needs of students at a relatively early stage in their education, because it does not provide them with a sufficiently broad overview of the continuity of history. But thematic and chronological models should not be regarded as mutually exclusive; they can be sensibly and productively combined without reducing historical narratives to fragmented foci of analysis punctuated by puzzling chrono-logical gaps.

A parallel but related debate concerns the search for the signifi-cance of the term 'Europe' itself in historical terms. There has been an implicit assumption that the insertion of the 'European dimen-sion' in historical education between the 'national' and the 'global' is justified on the basis of a shared cultural heritage, and this can be reproduced as a continuous narrative stretching back to ancient times. There might be interesting and enlightening assumptions underpinning this particular model, even from an educational point of view, in the face of the political, socio-economic and cultural convergence of 'Europe' since the end of the Second World War. But how flexible or meaningful is this version of a common 'European' heritage when dealing with historically 'peripheral' cases, or with conceptualising divergent models? For example, the position of Russia or of the Ottoman Empire within this grand 'European' scheme remains extremely problematic for the coherence and plausibility of this uniform cultural model. In many cases, 'Europe' is implicitly or even directly equated with its 'Western' provinces – a distinction that goes as far back as the time of the division of the Roman Empire into Eastern and Western, the distinction between capitalism-feudalism, enlightenment-autocracy or, more recently, liberalism-socialism. But the horizontal axis of historical education does not necessarily revolve around similarities or shared values and trajectories. Perhaps the most conspicuous element of a distinct 'European' dimension lies in the astounding diversity and particularism that can be found in the wider European context. The danger with any grand narrative of 'European' historical trajectory is that it might rest on a restrictive rendition of the past, that could be accused of being as misleading and as arbitrary as the various ethnocentric schematisations of national histories.

In the end, the insertion of the 'European' historical dimension into the conventional dichotomy between ethnocentric and inter-national historical narratives raises a fundamental educational question about the best approach to relating the 'European' per-spective with both the 'national' and the 'global'. The 2001 Pro-gramme of the French Presidency in the Domain of Education stressed that

> It is our responsibility. We who want to build this Europe united in its diversity, to make certain the psychological intellectual and affective foundations of political Europe. It is up to each member state not only to create within its own frontiers a new state of mind which will make of our citizens, from their most tender age, European citizens, but also to deploy the means by which this identification may happen (Text of the address by Jack Lang and Lean-Luc Mélenchon, 'For a European desire to live together', part of the Programme of the French presidency of the European union, Division of Education, 2001)

The professed link between the 'broadening of the European dimension of education' and the objective of promoting a sense of parallel European citizenship provides planners of national curricula with a unique opportunity to define the meaning of and methodology for this project. The same EU document stresses that 'Europe is, for all of us, the echo-chamber between our nations and the world at large'. This suggests promoting a dual change through the various history curricula – on the one hand, abandoning the insularity of ethnocentric narratives without succumbing to an abstract, exaggerated idea of a 'European' common heritage that obfuscates national, regional and local diversity; on the other, bringing the global dimension closer to the experiences of young people through the lens of Europe's influence and role on the world stage. Teaching non-European developments from a European viewpoint may extend the knowledge of the students and stimulate their comparative insight, promoting at the same time a better understanding of the current trend of multiculturalism in Europe. But more importantly, it might also be a highly effective tool to positively promote of the meaning of European citizenship, through comparisons with vastly different cultural models around the world and underlining the crucial convergence of intellectual, cultural and political developments of what today constitutes 'Europe'. At the heart of a constructive, multi-layered historical narrative is the need to find and promote an effective balance between identifying unifying themes and enhancing comparative 'European' diversity – and, through this, a respect for 'complementary talents and characteristics'.

Given that responsibility for promoting these educational objectives lies within the realm of *national* strategies and decision-making, there will have to be a plurality of paths to achieve the broadening of the European dimension in education. Once again, this should be viewed as a strength, originating from national/ regional/local/cultural particularism, and not as a deficiency. European citizenship complements and does not antagonise existing allegiances to established or recently formed communities (be that nations, localities or minority identities). Advancing such loyalties in tandem presents planners of history curricula with the task of finding the most suitable themes and formulas for their audience. A comparative discussion of colonialism, for example, might be more appropriate for students in countries where colonial pursuits played a much more significant historical role in defining the national historical trajectory (Western Europe) but might be of less relevance in areas that were not directly affected by this discourse (Eastern Europe, the Balkans). Similarly, discussing the experience of living under a 'totalitarian' system of rule holds a much more particular relevance for the countries of the former socialist bloc in Eastern Europe – and especially those that endured the transition to post-communist reality through the devastating path of a civil war as in the former Yugoslavia. This understandable and highly creative consideration does not re-legitimise ethnocentricity. As stressed earlier in this chapter, rigid ethnocentric approaches prevents narratives from entering a hard core of conventional wisdom, reproduced more or less uncritically and without the bene-fit of insight into other viewpoints or the determination to make painful concessions about national past. In this respect, the teaching of such distressing historical experiences of international conflict, such as the Second World War, should be particularly targeted by planners of national history curricula – as it has been, with largely encouraging results so far – in order to develop strong com-parative insights without reproducing divisive chauvinistic dis-courses or traditional, unreformed 'establishment' views of national history.

A primary emphasis on a history 'from above' – government decision-making, wars and antagonisms – cannot generate a con-structive educational platform for advancing the 'European' perspective on historical education, however understandable and inevitable this system might be. Since the 1960s there have been impressive methodological developments within the discipline of history that have crucially re-defined the ways in which the past can be organised and constructed. The establishment of 'history from below', not simply as an alternative to the top-heavy traditional narratives, but as a crucial supplement to conventional views of history, has underlined the significance and suitability of new foci of historical interest. Social history, accounts of everyday life in given historical periods and places, the history of ideas, cultural theory, gender and oral history, as well as interdisciplinary approaches such as environmental history (see, for example, *The European Dimension in Teacher Training, Activity Book 2: An Introductory Course on Intercultural Cross-curricular Themes: National Curriculum, Environmental Issues* (Antonouris, 1990)) – to mention but a few new directions – have strengthened the horizontal axis of historical interpretation and for this reason are far better suited to generate and cultivate the impression of a shared 'European' historical trajectory. New parallel loyalties, such as gender, sexuality, ideology and ecology cut across the old taboo frontiers of ethnicity and statehood, thus promoting a new version of history that is *de facto* trans-national. In an increasingly multi-cultural and post-material European environment the significance of the nation may not be diminishing in psychological terms; but national images can no longer command the exclusive allegiance of a substantial number of individuals and groups in contemporary Europe. This is a fundamental change that should be acknowledged and addressed by history curricula in positive terms, that underline the relevance of the wider 'European' discourse to the lives of young people.

Examining textbooks, there are notable divergences across Europe. In some countries, for example Greece, textbooks continue to be uniform and the notion of further reading is still relatively novel. Even with primary sources incorporated into the text, decisions made at the level of production limit the horizon of the student. By contrast, many other countries have made substantial efforts to democratise and devolve the process of textbook selection, by allowing a larger degree of choice. In general, history textbooks are a reflection of the quality and openness of the general academic debate about the course of national history. The more the academic discourse is responsive to genuine revisionist reassessments, the easier will such views gradually find their way into school history textbooks, and the more teachers will be intellectually equipped to complement the textbook with additional information and view-points. The existence of a clear 'majority view' of national history, defensive towards critical reassessments and categorical in its main ideas, impedes the permeation of new ideas into the conventional narrative. At the same time, the domestic political conjuncture is of decisive importance in the reappraisal of conventional historical views. Greece is again a good example, in the sense that conventional anticommunist feeling had, until the early 1980s, blocked the re-writing of the history of the Second World War.

In France the political leverage of Gaullism until the early 1980s had rendered a critical reassessment of the French resistance difficult. In Germany, the radical revisionist views of Fischer in the 1960s manifested the resistance of traditional nationalist-minded historiography to ideas, which were barely flattering to the long-term trends of national history. Only open and receptive debate, however acrimonious, can pave the way for a more constructive re-articulation of history. The pace of this process varies across Europe and has to be accompanied by institutionalised interaction between historians from various countries. The 1951 French-German educational agreement has found worthy disciples in the following decades across Europe, allowing for the production of far more dispassionate and multi-layered narratives on aspects of what may be called 'uncomfortable' national past. The expansion of exchange programmes within the European Union have allowed both teachers of history and students at various levels of their education to acquire a broader view of educational practices and historical discourses across the continent. Trans-national initiatives, such as the *Network of Training Institutions* (RIF) and the *Multilateral School Partnerships* (MSP) – see the European Commission document: *Profiles of the RIF Sub-Networks – Network of Training Institution, Profils des sous-réseaux du RIF – Réseau d'Institutions de Formation* (Luxembourg: Office for Official Publications of the European Communities, 1994) – and the various exchange programmes of the EU (such as ERASMUS), have made a significant contribution to enhancing mobility within the European Union – not just of human resources and audiences but also of ideas and perspectives that have enriched the framework of historical education (cf. *European Research Group on Training for School Exchanges*

(ERGTSE), *Teaching for Exchanges – Aims and Ways of Teacher Training. Encounters for Training. Training to Encounter,* Strasbourg: Council of Europe, 1993).

'Whoever remembers history seems condemned to repeat it', wrote Claus Offe in 1996 in the shadow of the resurgence of aggressive ethnocentric nationalism in post-communist Yugoslavia. It is the responsibility of those involved in the formulation and delivery of national curricula to ensure that history serves as a constructive reminder of what should be avoided and what should be remembered, rather than as an imprudent incitement to live in the past and nurture the same forces of ethnocentricity that animated its bleakest moments. The development and reinforcement of the 'European dimension' in historical education has so far proved an invaluable resource in mitigating such ethnocentric narratives, and in making students aware of the exciting pluralism inherent in multi-faceted comparative or thematic historical narratives that transcend the insularity of conventional perspectives on national history.

But the function of a truly 'European' perspective on historical education extends far beyond a primarily defensive counteraction to biased ethnocentric narratives. Since the establishment of the 'European dimension' as a priority in the educational strategies of the European Union in the late 1980s the teaching of history has acquired a new, autonomous significance in direct relation to the promotion of European *citizenship* amongst young people. The solidification of this plural sense of belonging inevitably has to pass through the awareness of both cultural achievements *and* uncomfortable accounts (such as the Second World War), national/regional diversity *and* shared heritage, particularism *and* convergence. In this sense, the scope for innovation and bold interpretations as to how historical education may fit constructively into this novel framework remains stimulatingly wide and challenging.

**Note**

1.  *Resolution of the Council and the Ministers of Education meeting within the Council of 24 May 1988 on the European Dimension in Education,* Official Journal of the

European Communities, no. C 177, 6–7–88 (Luxembourg: Office for Official Publications of the European Communities, 1988). Cf. *Report on the Implementation of the Resolution of the Council and the Ministers of Education meeting within the Council of 24 May 1988 on the European Dimension in Education* (Brussels: Commission of the European Communities, 1993).

# 5

# Becoming political in different countries

Carole L. Hahn

Educating children and young people for democratic citizenship requires a particular kind of citizenship education – one that prepares them for the specific requirements of democracy. That is, democratic citizens-in-the-making need to acquire the knowledge, skills, and attitudes for participatory decision-making and for a way of living that respects diversity. In recent years there has been much interest in different countries about how to improve citizenship education (Torney-Purta, Schwille and Amadeo, 1999). Policy makers and teachers, who want young people to become knowledgeable, committed, and caring citizens, are asking which curriculum and instructional practices are most effective in reaching that goal. I believe that a comparative perspective can be helpful in that search.

By looking at citizenship education in different countries, one can reflect upon alternative practices and consider their consequences in varied settings. That is not to say that what works in one setting will work somewhere else. Because educational practices are deeply embedded in and reflective of particular cultural contexts, they cannot be simply borrowed. Rather, a comparative perspective enables one to see previously taken-for-granted practices in one's own country with fresh insights, as well as to envisage possible alternatives.

For the past 15 years I have been studying citizenship education in five western democracies – the United States, England, Denmark, Germany, and the Netherlands (Hahn, 1998, 1999a, 1999b). I deliberately chose five countries that have much in common. They share similar levels of economic prosperity and have had universal suffrage for almost a century. And most important, their over-lapping histories, which include the Enlightenment Age and the Protestant Reformation have resulted in their sharing similar ideals of limited government, individualism, participatory democracy, and respect for cultural diversity. At the same time, these five countries have had quite distinct traditions regarding the preparation of children and young people for their roles as citizens of demo-cracies. Indeed, the longer I have spent studying citizenship educa-tion in different countries, the more I have come to appreciate that countries and cultural contexts matter. While educating young people for their roles as global citizens, we must realize that there is also much that is specific to particular countries. Government struc-tures and political institutions and processes vary across countries. Additionally, there are many differences in political histories, civic cultures, educational systems, and pedagogic cultures even in countries that we expect to be quite similar. Thus, citizenship edu-cation is one field that is affected by specific elements derived from particular local, historical, philosophical, and cultural traditions and yet, at the same time, it is influenced by shared global factors.

As a consequence of studying different countries' policies and prac-tices, I have come to believe that four components are necessary for effective citizenship education in democracies. Students need to:

- acquire knowledge through carefully planned instruction;
- debate about public issues and take decisions;
- engage in civic action; and
- develop a positive identification with local, national, regional, and global communities (Hahn, 2002).

Other chapters in this book address the fourth element in the European context, so in this chapter I focus on the other three, drawing on examples from the five countries in which I have been studying civic education (Hahn, 1998; 1999a; 1999b). Additionally, I draw on findings from the recent 28-nation study of civic education conducted under the auspices of the *International Association for the Evaluation of Educational Achievement*, better known as IEA (Torney-Purta, Lehmann, Oswald and Shultz, 2001). I focus on what teachers and schools can do to stimulate young people's political and civic learning. Here, I use examples primarily from my studies of 14- to 19-year-old pupils. Nevertheless, I believe these principles apply equally to education for pupils 7 to 14 as I have described in Hahn (2002).

We must keep in mind that students do not passively receive information and schools are not the only places for teaching and learning. Rather, children and young people actively construct meaning pertaining to the civic and political realms from a complex web of relationships that includes the family, peers, school, the media, and culture at large (Haste and Torney-Purta, 1992; Torney-Purta, *et al.*, 1999; 2001). Within this complex process, schools and teachers clearly can and do make a difference.

## Becoming political in five countries

From 1986 to 1996, I gathered information in 50 schools in five countries (Hahn, 1998). I administered questionnaires to 14- to 19-year-old young people in 1986 and again in 1993 for the purpose of measuring political attitudes. Additionally, I observed classes in which most education for citizenship was likely to occur. I interviewed teachers, and in 1992–96 I interviewed students. Although it was not possible for me to obtain nationally representative samples of students or schools, I did try to purposefully select schools that represented the different types of schools in each country, located in different regions of the country. For example, the sample in Germany contained students in *Realschulen*, *Gymnasien*, and *Gesamtschulen* in three different *Lander* (states). The English sample contained students from state schools in seven different counties and one British 'public school' (independent, fee-charging, boarding school). Unlike my study, the IEA study of civic education used nationally representative samples of 14-year-olds (Torney-Purta, *et al.* 2001). The IEA sample students completed surveys of knowledge, concepts, attitudes, and experiences in 1999.

At the time of my study, there were considerable differences in the expectations for citizenship preparation in the schools of the five countries. On the one hand, the Danish law for *folkeskoler*, which pupils attend from ages 5 to 15 or 16, emphasizes that the school should model democracy in order to prepare citizens for partici-patory democracy. The school ethos, as well as the curriculum, reflect that purpose. Schools in Germany and the United States teach the subjects of social studies (broadly) and civics or govern-ment (more particularly) for the purpose of 'making good citizens'. The wider school environment is also viewed as contributing to civic education in these two countries. The schools in the Nether-lands and England, in contrast, have traditionally put less emphasis on citizenship preparation. Although both countries have recently adopted new policies, their implementation has just begun and the effects of the changes are not yet known. As I describe alternative ways in which schools can foster the acquisition of civic/political knowledge, give practice in democratic deliberation and decision-making, and provide opportunities for civic action, I draw on my experiences in the various countries.

## Developing knowledge through deliberately planned instruction

In discussions about improving citizenship education, I have often heard educators on both sides of the Atlantic say things like, 'I don't mean students should study the 'structure and function' of institutions as in the old dry civics courses.' Nevertheless, it is clear that some deliberately planned instruction is necessary. One finding of the 28-nation IEA study is that civic knowledge is a predictor of students' intentions to vote as adults (Torney-Purta, *et al.*, 2001). In the United States, researchers studying the national assessments of educational progress (NAEP) in civics concluded that students who have had courses in civics/government are more knowledgeable than those who have not had such courses (Niemi and Junn, 1998).

In the United States, fewer than 20 percent of students are likely to have had a specific course in civics/government by the age of 14, the target age in the IEA study. However, approximately 85 per cent will have such a course before they graduate from high school, usually at about age 17 or 18 (Hahn, 1999b; Niemi and Smith, 2001). When they do study civics/government, students in the United States are most likely to study the Constitution, the Bill of Rights, and other amendments. They learn about the three branches of the federal government, the distribution of powers among the national, state, and local levels, and landmark Supreme Court cases. Furthermore, students are taught much political history and given information about political institutions and processes in their history and other social studies classes before they are 14-years old (Hahn, 1999b). Indeed, in the recent IEA study, 79 per cent of 14-year-olds in the United States said that they had studied the US constitution sometime during the previous year (Baldi, Perie, Skidmore, Greenberg and Hahn, 2001). Almost as many (75 per cent) reported studying Congress. Close to 68 per cent said they had studied the Presidency and the Courts.

In my visits to German schools I saw *Sozialkunde* and other social studies lessons for students aged 13 to 16 in which they studied government, political institutions and processes, and current political events. They studied basic law, learned about differences in political parties, and discussed local, national, and international political issues. Additionally, upper secondary school students preparing to take the *Abitur* examination took a course in social sciences in which they studied politics and international relations in considerable depth.

In Danish schools there is not a particular local or state curriculum guide that classes follow as they do in the United States or

Germany. Rather, within broad limits, students study topics they have chosen. From the time they are about 12, Danish *folkeskole* students study topics in their social studies classes which the class selects according to the required distribution of 25 per cent time for politics, sociology, economics, and international relations. For students who take social sciences at the *gymnasium* (ages 15/16 to 18/20) a similar distribution is expected. Additionally, throughout their years of schooling students have lessons in Danish history and culture that are related to civic and political life. I visited classes that had chosen to learn about the debates over the Maastricht Treaty, the war in Yugoslavia, elections, and many other topics from which they acquired political knowledge.

In contrast, in England, where until recently citizenship education was classified as a 'cross curricular theme,' students repeatedly told me that they had not studied politics or government in school. The exceptions to that was the small percentage of students aged 16–18 who took a course in Politics to prepare for an A-level examination. In the Netherlands in the 1990s, it was estimated that fewer than 10 per cent students were likely to have studied a unit on political decision making for an examination in *maatschappijleer*, or 'study of society.' When I asked young people in state schools in England and in a variety of schools in the Netherlands if they were interested in politics or government, they frequently replied by saying, 'it's too complicated to understand' (Hahn, 1998). Recent reforms in these two countries are intended to address this problem. English schools must provide instruction for political literacy as one component in their provision for citizenship, and Dutch students must now study a unit in political decision making in secondary school.

One essential component of democratic citizenship education is deliberately planned instruction in political knowledge, concepts, and skills. However, providing a curriculum and instructions alone is not sufficient. Education needs to be delivered in a manner that encourages students to actively construct meaningful knowledge and commit themselves to ideas. For that reason, I believe it is important for political and civic education to be issues-based and for students to be given many opportunities for reflective inquiry, discussion, and decision-making.

## Providing opportunities for issues investigation, discussion, and decision-making

At the heart of democracy lies the ideal of government by the people. Citizens acting directly, or indirectly through elected representatives, take the decisions that affect public life. Toward that end, citizens need the knowledge, skills, and attitudes for deliberation and decision-making. Children and young people need opportunities throughout their education to practice inquiry into public issues, to consider alternative policies, and to reflect upon the likely consequences of various alternatives. Numerous scholars have emphasized that a hallmark of democracy is that no topic should be closed to investigation. In democracies it is therefore especially important that young people have the opportunity to explore controversial or problematic social, political, and economic issues; anything else would be to adopt totalitarian practices (Hunt and Metcalf, 1968). Controversial issues present citizens of democracies with challenges as they are called upon to debate and take decisions with others, many of whom have different views and/or cultural perspectives. To do so, young democrats need much practice (See Engle and Ochoa, 1988; Evans and Saxe, 1996; Hahn, 1998; Parker, 1996, 2001). For a variety of reasons in different national contexts, teachers are often reluctant to give students the necessary opportunities for such investigation and dialogue (Cornbleth, 2001; Lister, 1991).

Despite that reluctance, there is considerable evidence that there are benefits to having students investigate and discuss public policy issues in supportive classroom climates. To operationalize the concept of a 'democratic classroom climate,' Ehman (1969) developed a Classroom Climate Scale aiming to measure the extent to which students perceived that their social studies teachers dealt with social problems, presented at least two sides to issues, took neutral positions on the issues under discussion, and encouraged students to express their own views in a supportive classroom atmosphere. In a series of studies conducted by Ehman and others in the United States, it was found that students who reported the most open classroom climates had the highest levels of political interest, and political efficacy (a belief that citizens can influence government decision making). They also had higher levels of political trust, a sense of citizen duty, and lower levels of cynicism than other students. Moreover, students who experienced a closed classroom climate in which teachers did not present multiple views on social problems and students did not feel comfortable expressing their views, reported low levels of political efficacy, participation, and citizen duty (for a summary of this research see Hahn, 1996, 1998).

An open classroom climate has been found to be important cross nationally. In the first IEA civic education study, conducted with nationally representative samples of young people in nine nations in 1971, researchers concluded that an open classroom climate was important to both civic knowledge and attitudes (Torney, Oppenheim and Farnen, 1975). Students who reported having opportunities to regularly participate in classroom discussions, in which they were encouraged to express their opinions, were more knowledgeable, more politically interested, and less authoritarian than other students. Similarly, in the recent IEA study of 14-year-olds in 28 countries, an open classroom climate was a predictor of both civic knowledge and the students' stated intentions to vote as adults (Torney-Purta, et al., 2001). In my study of civic education in five countries, perceptions of an open classroom climate correlated positively with political attitudes of interest, efficacy, and trust (Hahn, 1998). What is particularly interesting, I think, is the variety of ways in which educators in different countries engage students in democratic dialogue and decision-making.

In Denmark, children and young people engage in deliberation and decision-making about issues in their immediate school environment and those facing citizens in the wider national and international arenas. From 6 to 16, *folkeskole* pupils participate in class meetings in which they decide how to handle behaviour problems, plan class trips, and whether or not they should spend money on such things as repairing a bike shed or purchasing a refrigerator for class use. They also give advice to their representatives to the school council about issues concerning the entire school. As mentioned earlier, Danish *folkeskole* students also debate and decide on the topics they will study in social studies. Student deliberation and decision-making extends through the *gymnasium* years (approximately ages 16 to 19). Moreover the practice of debating about and deciding on the topics to study is not limited to social studies lessons. When I asked one group of *gymnasium* students if there were any subjects in which they did not make such decisions, they thought for a while and finally said, 'mathematics.' The students with whom I spoke were learning the skills of demo-cratic discourse by regularly engaging in such experiences while they considered public issues in their immediate school environ-ment. They also considered issues of national and international import in their social studies/social sciences classes. They did that when they investigated such issues as whether or not Denmark should ratify the Edinburgh revisions of the Maastricht Treaty or provide troops in international conflicts, or how to handle problems of video violence and abused children. The primary purpose of group research projects, class discussions of texts, and questions in oral and written exams were to give students practice in using an analytic social sciences method, not merely to develop an opinion on an issue.

In German social studies/social sciences classes I have observed the frequent use of a *Pro/Contra* strategy, in which students are asked to consider the arguments for or against a particular policy or the advantages and disadvantages of a position. For example, students discussed reasons for and against lowering the voting age from 18 to 16 in state elections, changing the asylum laws, pro-hibiting extremist groups, changing the law related to abortion, and controlling genetic engineering. In German schools, I also observed many classes in which students were reviewing and discussing articles from newspapers or news magazines about local, national and international issues.

Discussions of current news events are a frequent practice in many social studies classes in the United States. Although sometimes the 'discussions' are shallow recitations of what, where, and why an event happened, in other classes there are more in-depth explorations of issues. Several students told me that they had not been interested in politics or current events until they had a particular teacher who expected them to keep up with the news and talked about it with them in class most days. As a result they said they became politically interested and aware. This is a clear example of how one teacher can make a difference.

Another practice, which I observed in classes in different parts of the United States, was to have individual students research a topic in their school library for a civics/government course. The students were expected to write a report in which they described a problem, summarized their research, and in the conclusion expressed their opinion and gave reasons for coming to their decision. Topics for reports included capital punishment, gay rights, affirmative action, gun control, immigration policies, and euthanasia – clearly controversial public policy issues. But not all students are encouraged to investigate such controversial topics.

In the recent IEA study, 75 per cent of American 14-year-olds reported that they regularly discussed current events in their social studies classes (Baldi, *et al.*, 2001). Additionally, on the Classroom Climate scale, 85 per cent said that they were encouraged to make up their minds about issues, and close to 80 per cent said that they were encouraged to express their views in class. In contrast, only 69 per cent of students said that their teachers encouraged them to discuss political or social issues about which people had different opinions. In my study, students in the five countries were also less likely to say that they often discussed controversial political, economic, and social issues than to say they were encouraged to make up their own minds or express views – apparently on non-controversial matters (Hahn, 1998).

I also saw fewer examples of English and Dutch students being encouraged to investigate public policy issues in preparation for citizenship than in the other countries. Nevertheless, students in some schools in those countries did have experiences that were related to deliberation and decision-making. In two schools I visited in the Netherlands, students wrote research papers on public issues but they were not expected to give an opinion or propose a solution to the problem. Topics dealt with environmental issues, policies on abortion and euthanasia, and the rise of right-wing groups in Europe.

In English schools students are likely to confront a variety of social issues but without exploring the political dimensions of resolving those issues or connecting them to their role as a citizen. I observed students in personal and social education lessons doing exercises related to drug and alcohol abuse, equal opportunities and prejudice, and the Universal Declaration of Human Rights. In religious education or religious studies classes, students learned about Britain's multi-faith society and they discussed issues such as capital punishment, abortion, racism, and human rights. Geography classes dealt with environmental issues and foreign aid to the third world. School assemblies often contained moral messages, but in those instances, as with classroom topics, the emphasis tended to be on how individuals ought to behave. Moral or ethical behaviour was the focus of attention, rather than the preparation of young people for their roles as citizens of a democracy. It will be interesting to see if that emphasis shifts as the new citizenship education legislation is implemented in English schools in the years to come.

In my study of 'becoming political' I administered questionnaires to measure students' levels of political interest, efficacy, confidence and trust, as well as their perceptions of classroom climate and civic experiences. Additionally, I interviewed students about those topics. Taken together, the data revealed clear country differences that correspond to differences in schooling and the wider political cultures. Exposure to political content and opportunities to reflect upon and take decisions about social and political issues in school and society enabled students to construct views of themselves as active and committed citizens. The absence of such exposure and opportunities seemed to have the reverse effect.

Danish students indicated comparatively high levels of political interest and efficacy. They often followed the news and discussed it with family, friends, and teachers. Many Danish students in my sample said they tried to persuade others to agree with their views and exhibited a high level of political confidence. They participated in class decision-making and indirectly in school decision-making. They observed debates and engaged in discussions about a national referendum. Overall, the Danish students in my sample appeared to be the most politicized of the students in the study. They attend schools in which political participation and discussion is practiced and they live in a culture in which participatory democracy is emphasized.

German students in the study showed high levels of political interest in 1986 and moderate levels in 1993. Both samples indicated comparatively low levels of political efficacy and expressed a belief that citizens have little influence on policy making. Nevertheless, the German students in the study said that they would definitely vote and the ones with whom I spoke were well informed about public affairs. Both the school curriculum and the civic culture were characterized by political discourse. Yet, in observing political events on the media, many young people came to the conclusion that average citizens have little influence in the four to five years between election periods. In contrast, the United States students indicated comparatively high levels of political efficacy. They cited both contemporary and historic examples of citizens influencing government decision-making. They learned about citizen action in their social studies classes and they observed examples in their communities. The Dutch sample indicated comparatively low levels of political interest and confidence and very few said they ever discussed politics or current events with their friends. The Dutch students in the study observed similar attitudes and experiences among adults in their cultural environment. Again, school and cultural messages combined as young people con-structed ideas of citizenship.

In England, students who attended a British public school were interested in politics and current events, which they reported dis-cussing with family and friends outside school. The students in the study who attended English state schools (with the exception of a few 17- to 18-year-olds), however, expressed little interest in the political arena. They were not likely to have studied politics or government in school nor to have discussed how citizens engage with such issues. They tended to view politics as a contest between parliamentary parties and did not see citizens as having much influence on the process. For the most part they saw only MPs (on television) engaging in political discourse. The ethos of the inde-pendent boarding school and the expectations of upper-middle-class parents for political participation provided stimulus for participatory attitudes when deliberate political education was not part of the school curriculum.

The attitude for which there was the least divergence across countries was political trust. Sample students in all five countries tended to have a low view of politicians and government leaders. The young people cited examples of broken promises once candi-dates took office. Students in the United States, England, and Germany also cited political scandals that they had learned about in the media. They took these images into account in constructing their mental schema of political leaders. In the recent IEA study trust was measured in terms of trust in government institutions, such as parliament, local government, the police, and the courts. As individual country reports become available, it will be possible to see whether particular subgroups within each country, as well as students from various countries, have differing levels of trust in particular institutions. I would hypothesize that the treatment of those institutions in the school curriculum combined with their role in the wider cultural discourse will be reflected in students' views.

In the next section we go beyond teaching and learning about democratic institutions and processes and rights and responsibilities of citizens. We look at how schools and teachers can help students extend their learning to become actively engaged in democratic life.

## Encouraging civic action

Citizens of democracies do not just think and talk about public issues. They take actions to influence policy making and to improve the quality of life in their local communities, in their countries, and in the global society. Active, participating citizens follow public affairs in the news, write letters, e-mails, and try to persuade officials and fellow citizens to support particular policies in other ways. Sometimes they sign petitions, join demonstrations, and support boycotts to make their voices heard. They also vote and join voluntary organizations. Children and young people need opportunities to take actions that emerge from thoughtful studies of civic issues, so that they will learn how to be effective citizens in a democratic context. As it is, studies and actions are too often separated from one another in young people's lives.

In recent years there has been much interest in community service and service learning in the United States, England, and other countries. Community service usually refers to the kind of charity work that is carried out by voluntary groups to help others. Service learning is the term that is used when community service is tied to the instructional programme of schools. The goals of service learning include increasing student knowledge about issues, fostering self-esteem and a sense of responsibility for others, and developing social and academic skills (Wade, 1997). Although service learning sometimes has the potential to develop political and civic knowledge, skills, and attitudes, too often that potential is not realized (Hepburn, 2000). Indeed, young people who spend hours in volunteer activities are often alienated from politics and claim no interest in policy making.

In my school visits I saw students in different countries engaging in participatory experiences in student councils. Beyond that I saw isolated instances of students taking actions to address issues in the wider community. In England, students often raise money at school for a charity, such as the Cancer Society or Oxfam, to help people in third world countries. The Danish association of gymnasium student councils used to sponsor One Day of Work. Students would take a day from school to do jobs to raise money for a charity. One year the money went to refugees in Kashmir, another year to environmental protection actions in Brazil. In Germany, some students told me they worked with local environmental groups or tutored in a community centre serving refugees.

In Germany, I met students who had marched in demonstrations against racism. One year in the Netherlands, students said they had sent postcards against racism as part of a campaign sponsored by a local radio station. Also at one time, students said they had joined a day of protest against raising local bus fares. And in the Netherlands I met students in one school who, after studying about human rights, had written letters to leaders in Turkey about the treatment of the Kurds and to leaders in the United States expressing their objections to capital punishment.

In the recent IEA study, 50 per cent of 14-year-olds in the United States reported having participated in a voluntary association to help the community (this compared to 18 per cent internationally) (Torney-Purta, et al., 2001). Moreover, the activity that students in the United States were most likely to associate with being a good citizen was 'participating in activities to help in the community' with 89 per cent saying that it was important or very important. That compared to 83 per cent who thought that voting in every election was important. Even fewer said that following political issues in the media (66 per cent) and engaging in political discussions (58 per cent) were important (Baldi, et al., 2001). In a democracy, it is important that citizens are more than good neighbors. Democratic citizenship requires that citizens follow public affairs, express their views, and try to influence policies. A 'promising practice' that is being adopted by schools and after school programmes in the United States and England is to have students identify a problem in their community, investigate alternative solutions, and make a proposal to decision makers. (For information on such programmes, see the Websites for the Centre for Civic Education's Project Citizen, The Constitutional Rights Foundation's ACT programme, and Street Law's Youth Act!)

## Conclusion

Curriculum planners, teachers, and administrators can each play their part to provide students with opportunities to experience the full range of citizen behaviour. I have tried to provide examples from varied contexts to show how that can be done. But it is important to keep in mind that the components I have described separately need to be combined in a comprehensive programme. Each element is necessary, but not sufficient without the others. Providing opportunities for students to acquire knowledge, investigate public policy issues, take decisions and take actions, along with giving them opportunities to develop multiple identities of citizenship, go hand in hand. Finally, those experiences need to be multicultural and global in nature, if we want to adequately prepare students for 21st century citizenship.

# 6

# Attitudes towards European Union citizenship

## Dave Edye

This chapter examines issues surrounding the debate on European Union citizenship. The context of this debate is discussed first by outlining the ideas of some of the main protagonists, then analysing the way the Commission tries to find out about attitudes toward European identity and citizenship. Finally the chapter presents the findings of research that has been carried out in the last two years with young people in London, Montpellier and Barcelona. This looked at attitudes toward issues such as allegiance, identity and citizenship, particularly European Union (EU) citizenship. The research has involved a mixture of questionnaires, interviews and focus groups. The initial research was carried out in London among young people in three locations, a final year group of school students, divided into two gender groups, a group of students in a further education college and members of a community theatre group. The first project was directed towards 16- 18-year-olds. The second and larger project was aimed at 18- 25-year-olds in the three countries, although most of the respondents were 18- 19-years-old.

The underlying assumptions of the project were that, while citizenship refers to the identification of citizens with institutions, it also depends on a whole range of social attitudes connected with political participation, cultural practices, group identity and social values. This relationship between the formal aspects of citizenship and more deeply embedded allegiances means that a purely institutional approach fails to understand the deeply rooted attitudes that underlie participation (or non-participation) in political processes. Furthermore, these attitudes may be affected by differing local, regional and national contexts and this makes comparative research particularly important. Finally, it is particularly interesting – and significant for the future development of citizenship in Europe – to research the attitudes of young people.

Young people were selected because their expectations and attitudes will shape the future of Europe. They have had access to EU educational and cultural programmes and their view of the EU is not shaped by the historical accomplishments of the Common Market. In addition, many of them do not participate in the national political process, which renders their political allegiances unknown. London, Montpellier and Barcelona provide respectively a sample of northern Euroscepticism, post-Maastricht doubts at the heart of a founding member of the Community, and southern autonomic pro-integration. The bigger project addressed the failure of high-level concepts of citizenship in the European Union to engage people's beliefs and participation. It also related a similar distance in EU citizenship to the wider crisis of legitimacy experienced at the national level and in several other institutional contexts. The attitudinal, comparative information generated provides valuable input for policy making across these levels.

This project was innovative, because it focused on people's views of citizenship and allegiance, while using a different methodology from the *Eurobarometer* and other national surveys. In order to study people's attitudes and ideas, specific, more practical questions were asked that could be understood by citizens from different countries, social classes, ethnic groups, sex and age. Such questions must go beyond declared identification with one's country and opinions of European Union institutions, and include issues such as mobility, equal opportunities, and support for multicultural policies.

## The context

In the heyday of the nation-state, which authors, like Giddens (1991) argue is now coming to an end in the 'late modern age', citizens accepted or were given a secure and usually exclusive identity. This identity imposed on them an allegiance which could be mobilised in times of conflict to recruit or coerce them as defenders of the mother/father land. A challenge to this secure identity has arisen with the relative decline of the nation-state, the impact of globalisation via migration and diaspora, and the growth of some kind of supranational 'state' in the European Union (EU). The loss of a secure national identity has had an impact on feelings of belonging and on notions of citizenship. This link between national identity and citizenship has been recognised by many writers (Habermas, 1992; Delgado-Moreira, 1997; Colley, 1999; Castles and Davidson, 2000).

Colley, for example, distinguishes between identity and citizenship ... identity is 'more ancestral and visceral' whereas citizenship is 'political and functional' (Colley 1999:4). If the 'ancestral and visceral' nature of identity is no longer able to be grounded in the nation-state of which an individual is a member or resident, then this may well affect their sense of belonging and allegiance. It may, therefore, be necessary for the nation-state or the supranational state to ensure social cohesion by appealing to other more 'political and functional' means through a rights-based polity and political culture. Certainly the current attempt to construct Europe needs to include more than 'rather empty symbols' (Newman, 2001) that imitate a very traditional nation-state approach, through currency, a flag and an anthem (Shore, 2000). It is only recently at the Nice summit in 2000 that the EU has engaged itself in the first serious attempt to introduce a more explicit rights-based polity. There is a realisation that the project of European integration needs some kind of meaning other than that based on instrumental economic and commercial factors. The Convention on the Future of Europe may be able to reinvigorate both the purpose and meaning of further integration.

For writers like Habermas the answer lies in developing a sense of 'constitutional patriotism'. Despite recognising the very limited extent of citizens' rights as promoted by the EU, Habermas is cautiously optimistic. The examples of multicultural societies such as the United States and Switzerland are used to demonstrate that

> a political culture in the seedbed of which constitutional principles are rooted by no means has to be based on all citizens sharing the same language or the same ethnic and cultural origins.... in a future Federal Republic of European States, each national tradition will have to relate to other cultures and traditions, and be connected with the overlapping consensus of a common, supranational shared political culture of the European Community. Particularist anchoring of this sort would in no way impair the universalist meaning of popular sovereignty and human rights. (Habermas, 1992: 7)

Meehan, like Habermas, takes a guardedly optimistic view, referring to a concept of neo-imperial citizenship similar to the notion of citizenship during the Roman Empire. Likewise Soysal (1994) sees within the framework of the EU the potential for the development of a 'post-national citizenship'. Other writers are clear that 'citizenship should therefore not be connected to nationality (that is, to the idea of being one people with common cultural characteristics); citizenship should be a political community without any claim to common cultural identity'. (Castles and Davidson, 2000:24)

Aron (1974) and Grimm (1997) question whether such a European citizenship can develop. Aron argues that national and Community authorities provide a group of rights that are of a different order from one another. Furthermore citizens can insist that the nation-state respects their rights, while no multinational polity has the same authority. Finally, at the time of writing in the 1970s, Aron could discern no popular demand for a European federation with all the attendant implications of such a development. There still appears little demand for a European federation among the citizens of the EU but there may be the beginnings of a recognition that the EU must implement a more rights-based polity. For Grimm the idea of a meaningful common citizenship is premature as there is no

European *demos,* the political structures and processes are not developed and without a common language it will be difficult to envisage a European identity.

## To belong or not to belong? Can we research people's attitudes to European Union citizenship?

This section examines the research available on attitudes to citizenship in the European Union (EU). It focuses on the *Eurobarometer* polls and Constant Tracking Surveys (CTS), and in particular no. 47.2 in 1997, which was aimed at measuring young people's attitudes towards the EU. Attitudinal data may be considered too subjective for some research topics, but it is precisely the citizens' subjective views about EU citizenship that are most needed. Loyalties to countries and to the Union are affected by feelings, opinions and prejudice, which are best accessed through attitudinal qualitative research, and cannot be inferred from political economy. The research focuses on how responses to these various surveys and questionnaires reflect issues concerning consent (allegiance), and belonging (loyalty, identity).

This aspect of the research is relevant to the concerns of teachers and students at all levels since it aims to analyse the assumptions that are included in these mainly quantitative surveys. These surveys tend to ask broad questions regarding identity or citizenship, without unpacking the concepts and probing the realities behind these concepts.

Perhaps it is a revealing detail that the unit responsible for the *Eurobarometer* is called the 'Citizens' Centre'. It is part of the Directorate-General for Education and Culture and deals with different types of surveys:

The traditional *Standard Eurobarometer* (EB – established in 1973): ±1000 representative face-to-face interviews per member country carried out between two and five times per year with reports published twice yearly. In-depth studies are carried out for various services of DG Education and Culture (on their behalf and account) and likewise for any DG of the Commission needing them, as well as for other EU institutions (if and when they so wish, as Parliament regularly does).

The *Flash Eurobarometers* are conducted, by phone, throughout the EU if and when needed by a service of the Commission or other institutions/agencies of the EU. Possibilities are numerous: variable interview techniques, variable sample size, 'special target groups' (e.g. teachers, managers, opinion leaders, etc.) or 'public at large' studies. Here again, it is the responsibility of the respective services to release their results.

The *European Continuous Tracking Survey* (CTS) was carried out, for the Commission Services, from January 1996 until December 1998. It succeeded the small pilot telephone 'Monthly Monitoring' created in 1994. The CTS consisted of some 200 telephone interviews done in each Member State, each week, 44 weeks a year. These results were regularly published in *Europinion* reports until the end of 1997. A special edition, European Public Opinion on the Single Currency, was also released in January 1999.

The *Central and Eastern Eurobarometer* (CEEB) was an annual general public survey which had been organised from 1990 to 1998. In the course of the year 2001, the Commission launched a new instrument, the Applicant countries *Eurobarometer*, modelled on the *Standard Eurobarometer*. The survey was carried out in the 13 candidate countries (www.europa.eu.int/comm/dg10/epo/org.html).

The *Eurobarometer* (EB) is the benchmark for researching European citizens' attitudes. The exact questions asked have changed over time, some have been added from time to time to focus on a particular subject, while basic questions about European integration have featured in all *Eurobarometers.*

The first finding is that citizenship was not included in the *Eurobarometers* until several years after the Maastricht Treaty, whereas allegiance to the European Union interpreted as 'feeling European' was one of the staple questions of the *Eurobarometer* and has been asked in the years preceding Maastricht.

*Eurobarometer 44* (1995) saw the inclusion of questions about the regions and a federal structure for Europe. The question on the level of attachment to different regional entities was new and has not been used again until April 1999 (EB 51), perhaps due to the fact that allowing respondents to choose identification has relegated the feeling of *Europeanness* to a distant fourth, behind nationality, region and locality. We had to wait until 1996 to see a clear concern with citizenship. In 1996, EB 45 included several sections dealing with citizens. The second section profiled European Union citizens and included an interesting typology of attitudes to European integration. Such a typology was based on a factorial analysis of 161 variables, and yielded 20 factors, which lead to four types. Preoccupation with national identity and culture is one of those factors, but the variables asking explicitly about citizenship are not.

The presence of citizenship in the *Eurobarometers* has been maintained and refined, but after EB 47 it has ceased to have a separate chapter. EB 46 (conducted in November 1996) placed the questions included in EB 45 – chapter 7 in the different context of 'Media usage and the rights of citizenship'. The variable information about EU issues had been used much earlier, but this was the first time it was used specifically regarding citizens' rights. *Europinion 10* (January 1997, Continuous Tracking survey) also included several questions about immigration, which allowed for further elaboration on the trust variable and the diversity aspects of citizenship.

*Eurobarometer 47* served as the basis for two other reports on young people's and women's attitudes to the European Union, published in December 1997 and March 1998 respectively, in addition to *Eurobarometers 47.1* (Racism and Xenophobia in Europe) and *47.2* (Young Europeans). *Eurobarometer 48* (1998) included a section 6 on the European Year against Racism, which asked about acceptance of cultural difference.

## Acceptance of people from non-EU countries

The next point is related to the study of attitudes toward foreigners and people of different ethnicities, including a new question on the acceptance of people of another culture/nationality (not disturbing, disturbing).

EB 48 must be read in conjunction with EB 47.1 'Opinion poll: Racism and Xenophobia in Europe', which was requested by DGV of the European Commission. The report claims that no similar poll has been carried out since 1988.

EB 47 included 23 questions for 15- 24-year-old respondents, which were analysed in EB 47.2 on Young Europeans (Melich, 1999). This group of questions was innovative in several respects, since it used an accessible language in the options given, and was open to spontaneous questions allowing several answers. For example when asking: Which of the following statements best describe(s) what the European Union means to you personally? Some of the options were: 'a way to create a better future for young people ', but also 'a lot of bureaucracy, a waste of time and money'. Original questions were included such as:

- Forecasts of the development of the EU: 'Taking everything into consideration, what will the European Union have brought in ten years' time?', with one of the options being 'There won't be a European Union anymore'.

- Discrimination: 'Do you feel uneasy in the presence of any people in your daily life?' In this case the options were people of another nationality, ethnicity, religion, but also physically or mentally handicapped people, homosexuals, drug addicts, or people who dress differently from you.

- Obstacles to mobility: 'Let's suppose you wanted to work or study abroad, what, do you think, would be the main difficulty you would face? Options included: I would not know how to find a job, language difficulties, administrative difficulties, I'd be homesick, or I am not interested in working or studying abroad.

## Support for EU policies, issues of priority and subsidiarity (take action or not)

From EB 49 and 50 (1998) up until the most recent one, EB 53 (2000), citizenship is addressed as a matter of information and knowledge of the European Union. These *Eurobarometers* devote considerable space to current policy issues such as enlargement and the euro. But simultaneously, more specific questions appear that link citizenship with the democratic process.

As mentioned earlier, statistical analyses were conducted to identify attitudinal groups among young people and women. In this case, the underlying concepts in 52 questions (or variables) were isolated through Principal Component Analysis, leaving us with the following 18 concepts. The actual labels are the analyst's invention, but the statistical analysis produces groups of like-minded responses, patterns of responses. In the study on young people three groups were found: sympathisers (38 per cent), sceptics (28 per cent) and positive pragmatics (33 per cent). The relevant clusters of women's attitudes were five: sympathisers (25 per cent), sceptics (19 per cent), pragmatics (20 per cent), 'middle-of-the-roaders' (14 per cent), and indecisive persons (22 per cent). This type of analysis also permits to build a profile by the variables available in the data file, i.e. sex, age, nationality, political identification, etc. According to this analysis, these are the factors that best distinguish attitudinal groups among a class of people. If we take together the analysis carried out on young people and women, then we have a complete list of the concepts which have explained variance between groups among women and young people: a good indication of how the population could fare.

## What is a European Citizenship question?

We have selected some questions as relevant to the attitudes towards EU citizenship, even though they did not explicitly contained the expression 'EU citizenship', or were not included under a citizenship heading by the EB. For example, we selected questions about employment, immigration and racism. What was the criterion? This is the key problem of the definition of citizenship as a survey variable. Every researcher has to make informed and theoretically sound decisions as to what citizenship is about, and then proceed to break it up into variables and design appropriate questions.

Not surprisingly, though all six countries studied have used a certain number of common questions on European integration, there are substantial differences between the European questions in their domestic surveys. The surveys reviewed show different priorities and agendas for European integration in different countries. For example, only the French surveys give their respondents the choice between a Federal Europe and a Europe of Nations, as in the CSA Opinion-France Inter exit polls conducted on 13/06/99. Only questions found in the Swedish questionnaires ask the respondents whether their opinion toward the euro would be influenced by the decision of a second country (Denmark; SIFO survey, 1999). We have not found anywhere else a national survey linking the behaviour of citizens of two member states. Furthermore, the German surveys are the only ones to ask about the pride of being European, about Europe as a fatherland, but also about more specific things such as payment of pensions abroad, the harmonisation of motorway tolls, and key institutional issues such as the hierarchy of competences (who has the final competence for environmental protection). Only the UK fails to give the possible answer of European feeling when surveying its citizens on feelings of nationalism (*British Social Attitudes survey*, 1999).

The long-standing use of the *Eurobarometer* in all the countries studied, except in Sweden, allows a comparison of the responses to a common set of questions. We have argued that the *Eurobarometer* has studied citizens' attitudes to a very wide range of European issues. However, not all of these questions allow us to understand people's allegiances. For example, it is doubtful that degrees of awareness about how much of the EU budget is spent in the Common Agricultural Policy can help us study allegiances. And yet that question was used in the factorial analysis of *Eurobarometer*

*45* (1996). Hence, we have focused on citizens' attitudes to citizenship.

In this sub-group of European attitudinal research, we are left with the questionnaires designed and the data gathered by *Eurobarometers*. The 1998 Runnymede Trust and Commission for Racial Equality survey in the UK and the 1994 CIS survey on European feelings of the Spanish people stand out as those most focused on feelings of belonging and European identity among the domestic studies. These two studies concentrated on loyalty as the key underlying theory that describes the relationship between individuals and government. Accordingly, they ask about 'images' of Europe, of the self, and of the national community. Not surprisingly, the loyalty to Europe scores very low levels. A theoretically inspired criticism of this approach is that there is a mismatch between the nature of the relationship between citizens and Europe and the theory of emotional loyalty to an institution. The latter was largely developed in the 19th century to rally support for the nation-state projects, and has been buttressed ever since by a mandatory common language and a mass education/religious system. The distilled product is 20th century emotional loyalty. This should not be a surprise, but the natural hypothesis derived from a widespread understanding of the nation-state project. Moreover, if that system had been completely successful, then the proportion of people who embrace Europeanness alone (the alternative hypothesis), given these types of questions, could not be more than 5 per cent, a standard level of statistical confidence.

We can safely conclude that something is wrong with this hypothesis, in light of the fact that those who regard themselves more as Europeans are 42 per cent among Italian youths, and 21 per cent in British youths, leaving Germany and France in between, according to the latest MORI survey for *Time Fortune* (*Time*, April 2, 2001; p. 46). Defenders of the loyalty model will claim that they still command the majority of the population, or that emotional attachment and loyalty can be shared on a number of levels. But they will be advised to be careful. While it is true that the levels of

Europeanness drop dramatically when asking people to pick a first and second geographic space if they are given the option of identification with their local towns and cities, the levels of identification with the nation also drop. For example, an above average pro-European country such as Spain scores only 1 per cent of respondents who select Europe as their first level of geographic identification, and only 4.3 per cent do it as second (1994 CIS survey on European feelings), but the rate of 'national' (i.e. Spanish) identification also plummets and the unified loyalty is shattered.

A similar predominance of the national level is one of the key limitations of the *Eurobarometer* to test the loyalty hypothesis. Every variable is presented by country, and complementary analysis by federal states or by regions is not supplied. Indeed, one could safely assume that this is not made available by the survey agencies, even though they should have used them in sampling.

As far as the practical meaning of European citizenship in *Eurobarometers*, DG X of the Commission has supplemented the loyalty model by following the Marshall evolutionary, rights-based definition of citizenship as consisting on civil, political and economic rights. Hence, the first question regarding citizenship that becomes a staple question is 'feeling European', with choices that exclude identification with regions and towns. We have argued that only from 1996 did a wider concern with citizenship emerged. Then, the second most common citizenship question concerns awareness of citizens' rights (civil/political citizenship), and reliability of institutions of government (political citizenship) which evolves into questions of access to information about citizens' rights (particularly dominant in the period 1998–2000). The loyalty model, which so dominated citizenship questionnaires in Europe, could also be seen in the introduction of questions about fears (negative expectations for the future), trust (between peoples as in EB 46, of immigrant groups as in *Europinion 10*, 1997), and acceptance of cultural difference (EB 48, 1998, including section 6 on the European Year against Racism).

Of course, although there have been questions in *Eurobarometers* about employment and social and economic rights, we are merely describing the fact that they have not been linked with citizenship. Furthermore, the re-focus of citizenship questions on issues of access to information and the media seems to suggest that European citizenship risks becoming an even more soft-core Public Relations concern in the age of the Internet.

This linkage between questions that explicitly tackle citizenship and issues that are related but are not presented as citizenship provides us the opportunity to put more interesting theories to the test. Even within the loyalty view, also known as the national-liberal model of citizenship, of which all west European countries participate to a large extent, some interesting relationships should be explored. The detail of the social and demographic questions asked by the Spanish surveys on the European Union would allow a researcher to cross-tabulate the feelings of attachment to the locality/province/nation/Europe with actual places of birth, there-fore telling us whether sub-state nationalisms are or are not pro-European and in what sense. Moreover, the variable 'feeling European' could be cross-tabulated with socio-economic status, to explore if it is only the upper classes who feel European while the worse off live in fear of cheap imports and globalisation. Only the *British Social Attitudes Surveys* and the ISSP 1995 National Identity in Germany have a design comparable to the Spanish ones and include such socio-demographic variables. Yet alas the former is not too concerned about identification with Europe, so that we do not have the 'feeling European' variable in that data-set. The factorial analysis conducted in EB 47.2 tells us what types of attitu-dinal profiles can be found across Europe, but their ultimate theoretical and empirical relevance is limited. What are we to make of the fact that 14 per cent of European women have an attitudinal profile labelled 'middle-of-the-roaders'? Though there is nothing more practical than a good theory, the idea behind this attitudinal profiling is not very practical.

We could use statistical analysis to test other theories of the relationship between individuals and the state. Let us assume Van Kersbergen's (2000: 5) definition of allegiance, which follows Milward's (1997) in a utilitarian way as 'the willingness of a national public to approve of and to support the decisions made by a government, in return for a more or less immediate reward to which the public is entitled on the basis of it having rendered approval and support'. Even without the benefit of designing *ad hoc* questions, we could cross-tabulate the subjective assessment of whether a country has benefited from EU membership with the opinion on the best level of political responsibility for certain policies. Ideally, the EB should make more specific questions under the umbrella of the overall 'benefit from EU membership', so that answers on the benefit to a country from EU membership in health and social welfare could be cross-tabulated with support to European level of political responsibility in social affairs. Utilitarian allegiance would have us predict that a given benefit from EU membership should correlate positively with support for European responsibility in that policy field. Unlike in the loyalty/identity theory, the *Eurobarometer* is not designed in a way that allows an easy test 'off-the-shelf', but our hypothesis is that the relation between the two will not be statistically significant in areas of social and economic policy. It would be partly easier to test in a similar way the relationship between the actual political participation of citizens in their local, national and European institutions and their support for certain forms of institutional reform. We are not thinking about simple voting patterns, but of cross-tabulating questions about the perceived importance of the European Parliament in the future and agreement with the statement 'the European Commission should have support from the European Parliament'.

Unfortunately, sociological imagination alone will not be able to squeeze as much out of the data currently available as if theories of citizenship had influenced the design of the questionnaires. For that, we can list examples of the best practices that we have encountered. Together with the theoretically inspired hypothesis-testing outlined above, they should ensure that surveys become much more productive.

The reason why the *Eurobarometer* provides the benchmark for European opinion is because it is run by DG X of the European Commission, perhaps the only institution in the world genuinely concerned about European public opinion. Having reviewed the questions, one cannot help a feeling of dismay at the answers. EB 47.1 opened by stating that the survey shows a worrying level of racism and xenophobia in member states, with nearly 33 per cent of those interviewed openly describing themselves as 'quite racist' or 'very racist'. In the same special report, the EU15 average of opinion about the institutions and political establishment shows that only 24 per cent have a positive opinion, while 43 per cent have a negative one and the remaining 33 per cent a critical one. Finally, EB 52 (published in April 2000) shows that the EU average support for EU membership has remained almost flat between 1981 and 1999, except for a peak in 1991. It is currently 51 per cent, reportedly up from 50 per cent earlier in 1999. Those who think membership is a bad thing have been the same in number since 1981 at 13 per cent, and those who think it is neither good nor bad have not changed either over the past 20 years and account for 27 per cent of the opinion. In other words, the EU might even lose a EU-wide referendum about EU membership, particularly since the likely turnout could be just 57 per cent (the average in 1999 European Parliament elections).

The conclusion is that citizenship sits at the crossroads of problems in its two dimensions: politico-constitutional, where people's participation in their democratic institutions is conspicuous by its absence; and identity/multicultural: where people's allegiance to their local groups and their high levels of racism and xenophobia do not prevent a boring social life.

That is why in addition to snapshots of what people think of the status quo, we should explore the process of opinion formation and the relationship between variables that people themselves make, not those that we can derive from our secondary analysis. Only by probing in this way can we understand the nature and the likely outcome of this wave of 'watchful consent'.

Moreover, questions concerning attitudes must be theoretically contextualised, or else the investigators are working intuitively.

## Three country survey

We now outline the findings from the pilot research project on young people and citizenship in London, Montpellier and Barcelona, in which they were asked to reflect on their own sense of belonging and their attitudes towards citizenship at local, national and supranational levels. Purposive sampling was used to select the groups in all three centres (cf. de Vauss, 2000).[1] More than 50 questionnaires were distributed in each centre (Response rate of around 80 per cent) and two focus groups were carried out in each centre between October and December 2001. A gender balance was achieved, but respondents came overwhelmingly mainly from the 18–19 age group and almost all were in full-time education.

Most of the following comments are based on analysis of questionnaire responses and the focus group sessions. All members of the focus group had completed the questionnaire either some time before the sessions or at the beginning of the session before discussion took place. The discussions were structured initially around responses to the questions. The qualitative data from the focus groups was analysed using QSR and the quantitative data from the questionnaires using SPSS.

The questionnaire was divided broadly into three parts, the first section on personal background, networks and identity, the second on political participation and citizenship and finally some questions on European citizenship.

## Personal Background, Networks and Identity

Our initial hypotheses were that people are more or less comfortable with a notion of multiple identity as a way of self-definition. The research has borne this out with a great deal of cross-cutting reference points in terms of identity. Less than 10 per cent of the respondents referred to a mono-identity just in terms either of local (city), regional, national or European identity. Most people had either come from another part of the country to these cities, or from abroad (c.10 per cent), and many had family dispersed in other EU and non-EU countries. In both Montpellier and Barcelona more than 60 per cent of the population originates from outside the city. Furthermore, many of the respondents kept contact by phone or Internet with friends in other parts of the EU and further afield. The importance of networks is highlighted by the research, which extends beyond family and local place.

On the other hand, home as the primary locator in terms of belonging is important, but it is problematic. Home is where the family actually is, but also in the first London focus group there was the idea that 'real' home is back there in the origin of the diaspora. This can be seen either as a dynamic feature of multiple identity, or as a source of tension between actual home here and now and a preferred home imagined somewhere else. One of the respondents in the first French focus group expressed a similar feeling of preferred home, located not where his immediate family was now but where his family came from in his grandparents' region. Furthermore a London respondent had never been to her parents' homeland.

Although London respondents felt more strongly attached to their city than the others, the majority response in all cases was a lack of any strong identification with the city. On the other hand, those who expressed a moderate attachment to their city also felt they had more in common with other EU citizens. 46.7 per cent of London respondents felt European, compared to 70 per cent of those in Montpellier and 61 per cent in Barcelona. However over half of the respondents in all three countries felt that people would feel more

European in 10 years' time (London 51.5 per cent, Montpellier 60.5 per cent and Barcelona 85.2 per cent).

There was no specific question on allegiance, but we can infer from respondents in all three countries that allegiance to the nation-state in which they live is problematic. This was most obvious in Barcelona but it was also prominent in London and Montpellier.

European identity is often defined in terms of the Other. Europe is perceived by both the London and Barcelona groups as being over there. Furthermore, in Montpellier and Barcelona, people defined Europe as more 'open' and more 'progressive' than the United States and expressed quite strong hostility towards the United States. There was, however, on the whole, a positive attitude towards the idea of the construction of a European identity, linked to a notion of European citizenship (see below).

## Citizenship

For the London groups, citizenship is defined in terms of active participation in the community and local politics. This is almost a good neighbourly idea rather than the far more explicit notion of rights that is expressed by both the Montpellier and Barcelona groups. Furthermore, this rather hazy, rather cosy feeling about the local community in London is not actually realised in any form of involvement either in terms of knowledge about local political processes or active participation in those activities. This is a general feature shared by all the groups.

Many people highlighted the individualistic nature of modern societies, which militates against more active participation and more social solidarity. Furthermore, the effect on social solidarity of job insecurity was also mentioned.

However a common theme uniting all groups is the feeling of alienation from the political process especially in so far as it affects young people. From the fact that there are no special mechanisms for young people to articulate their wishes to the recognition that they have very little say at any level of politics. 55.5 per cent said they had no say in how their city was run, 62.1 per cent said they had no say in how their country was run and 69 per cent said they had no say in how the EU was run. These findings are borne out by studies in the UK which indicate that age is the most powerful predictor of involvement in conventional politics (cf. Fahmy, *Young People's Participation*, results from 1996 MORI Omnibus Survey www.radstats.org.uk/no070/article3.htm). There is an active interest in major current issues but no real desire to become involved at any level in the traditional forms of political engagement. Political elites are considered as distant. They are all more or less corrupt and part of a media celebrity circus. Few respondents are members of local associations and voting is more prevalent at national than local elections. Voting is however undertaken by the majority of people but in a fairly lacklustre and mechanical way. These groups represent, therefore, a more committed group in terms of participation with the democratic process albeit at a very minimal level. The major problem remains of how to reconnect the political process with those who express widespread feelings of apathy, powerlessness and cynicism.

## European Citizenship

The meaning of European citizenship for most people was expressed very instrumentally by the fact that they could travel and work in other EU countries. There was little understanding, however, of the process whereby this had happened. It was presumed as a given, almost a right, which in one sense can be taken as a successful measure of European integration in that Europe's younger citizens now consider that they have a right to travel and work where they like within the Union. The long-term effects of freedom of movement may lead to a greater degree of interaction and therefore more sense of being European. This kind of process has been at the forefront of neo-functionalist ideas about spill-over. There is no compelling evidence, however, that such institutional processes have a great effect on people's sense of being or feeling European. There was on the whole a positive attitude towards the construction of a European space, but there was also a great deal of criticism of its overly economic rationale. From one of the Montpellier groups there was strong criticism of the EU as a neo-colonial enterprise in competition on a global scale with the USA.

In this context there were strong expressions of solidarity for immigrant groups and it was stated that they should be accorded full rights, including voting rights. Most participants were nationals of their respective countries, although there were a few non-nationals. There was also general agreement on the need for a more inclusive society. Most of the participants and respondents were well informed about key political, economic and social issues. There seemed to be a desire to engage with these issues but not through the established political process.

The findings of this survey are necessarily tentative given the sampling methodology and population size. There is, however, scope to make some assumptions about young people's ideas about the future of Europe in general and their place and role within it.

Most people feel a need to belong, and they are open to the idea of some kind of European identity. Although there was a positive attitude towards the construction of this identity it came more from a resigned acceptance rather than active involvement, as the process appears so distant. Nevertheless, all those who live in Europe, particularly immigrants and their families, should enjoy equal rights and so feel they also belong. This is important in terms of social cohesion. However people will only be held together on the basis of culture. And what kind of culture will that be? Will it be a common European culture which recognises diversity and how will this differ from the idea of multiculturalism, which evokes hostility in many parts of Europe?

A nation's collective memory gives rise to emotional ideas of belonging, related through common history, often dynastic, with numerous references back to mythic pasts or 'authentic' traditions. These ideas hold great sway over European populations. The success of extreme right wing parties all over Europe shows how powerful these ideas remain. At the same time emotional attachments to territory predominantly, and in one London case social class, are seen as stable anchors in uncertain times. These feelings need to be understood in light of basic human needs, despite the findings of the research which reveal that most of the respondents seem to be happy with the idea of multiple identity.

Dennis Smith considers that the EU can succeed if it can provide freedom (opportunity and autonomy), security (welfare and order) and respect (*The Times Higher Education Supplement*, 19 March 2002). Others may doubt the EU's sincerity in this process given, for example, its current attempt through the World Trade Organisation to force open to competition every public service provider in the world. This was the fear expressed by some of the respondents in the survey: that the EU would challenge the USA for global hegemony, with all the negative consequences of Empire.

Two approaches can be considered in overcoming the current malaise in the EU. The first approach begins through education and the second through reorganising the political structure and processes of the EU. Educators should give new kinds of civics classes, which implies giving up the search for common history and moving away from 'the Periclean warrior defence of cultural patrimony... and cultural predeterminations'. These classes should be based on exclusion of difference, and teach how to accept people at their face value. These Kantian marketplace values focus on low-level, weak systems of tolerance, trust, mildness and love (Castles and Davidson, 2000, pp. 218–219). The second approach requires the institutionalisation of a rights-based polity at the EU level which can reinvigorate the democratic process and lead to the creation of a strong 'democratic allegiance' (Newman, 2001, pp. 18–19). The aim is to achieve the seemingly impossible feat of finding the basis of a European identity that engages and has meaning for all its citizens.

# Note

1. 'Purposive sampling is a form of non-probability sampling where cases are judged as typical of some category of cases of interest to the researcher. They are not selected randomly. Thus a study of leaders of a conservation movement might, in the absence of clearly defined sampling frame or population, select some typical leaders from a number of typical conservation groups. While not ensuring representativeness, such methods can provide useful information'. (D. de Vaus, 2002, p. 90).

# 7

# The social and political learning needs of refugee students and asylum seekers from Third World countries in Irish post-primary schools

Maureen Killeavy

This chapter investigates the political and social learning needs of students who are refugees or asylum seekers seeking education in Irish post-primary schools. The number of students in this category and those who are classified as 'unaccompanied minors' has increased dramatically in the last decade. During this time the Irish economy has become so successful that the country has come to be known as the Celtic Tiger. This has resulted in the reversal of the traditional tendency for Irish people to emigrate in search of employment, a trend that was particularly marked in the 1980s. Apart from the return to Ireland of emigrants who had sought employment abroad, the last decade has seen the beginning of immigration to the state both from Eastern European countries and from the third world states. This changing pattern of migration, particularly the arrival of refugees seeking asylum in the country, has resulted in the Irish student population becoming increasingly multicultural. Some of these students arrive with their families while others, some of whom are teenagers, arrive unaccompanied. The study reported here is an investigation of the social and political learning needs of such students within the overall educational provision available to them in the state system. On the basis of the findings, suggestions for further research are indicated and recommendations are made.

## The educational provision for refugee students in post-primary schools in Ireland

Students arriving in Ireland from abroad who have been accorded refugee status, or who are either asylum seekers (post-July 1999) or unaccompanied minors, are entitled to the same educational provision at post-primary level as are Irish citizens. Non-EU students who do not fall into these categories are required to pay an economic fee for the courses they undertake. The provisions of the Education Act (1998) and the Equal Status Act (2000) promote equality of access and prohibit discrimination on grounds of race, skin-colour, nationality or ethnic origin. A further recent policy initiative, the White Paper on Adult Education (2000) *Learning for Life,* stresses 'the need to frame educational policy and practice in the context of serving a diverse population.' Together with access to regular educational provision, English language support for refugee children in post-primary schools can be arranged with funding from the Department of Education and Science. Refugee students may be provided with classes in mother tongue and cultural studies, as those initiated for Bosnian and Vietnamese students. However, there is no specific provision for social studies designed specifically for refugee students that would facilitate integration and social inclusion within school and community.

A large number of voluntary bodies and non-governmental organizations devoted to refugees and their needs have come into being in recent years, and some bodies also include refugee concerns in their remit: these include the Refugee Agency, Teacher Unions, Amnesty International, the Irish Centre for Migration Studies, the Conference of Religions in Ireland, and the Irish Refugee Council. Their work ranges from practical support for refugees and asylum seekers on a number of levels, to the pursuit of scholarly research and consciousness-raising activities. At a local level the practical support provided for refugee students involves such activities as the organisation of homework clubs and drop-in centres.

This study draws on the narratives and the activities reported by refugee students, with particular reference to their lives and their experiences of social activities after school hours. Their views on the political aspects of their current situation and their hopes and expectations are also explored. The purpose of the investigation was to ascertain these students' social and political learning needs, and to establish the extent to which they found the existing provision in this area accessible and relevant. The findings are discussed in the context of increasing European integration and citizenship.

## The design of the study

The investigation was based on qualitative research involving in-depth student interviews and projective techniques with a group of five male and one female student, all of whom were aged approximately sixteen. They were all currently taking post-Leaving Certificate and pre-university courses in a Dublin college. They lived in apartments in inner city areas of the capital. All members of the group were originally from African or Asian countries, and they have all been in Ireland for less than three years.

The perceptions and experiences of these refugee students were investigated using projective techniques. The interview schedule designed for the study paralleled the sentence completion instrument and it comprised a number of open-ended, loosely focused, questions. The interviews were recorded and content analysis was used to examine the views expressed by respondents in both the sentences they completed and in the recorded interview material.

## *Integration and inclusion: refugee students' experiences of social life in Ireland*

All the students reported identical experiences in Dublin of discrimination in public places, that mostly took the form of verbal

118

abuse. Sometimes this was accompanied by physical abuse, but respondents pointed out that the physical abuse they were subjected to during the daytime was rarely of a serious nature. In the evenings however, the situation became much more dangerous and it was considered unwise to venture out or visit places of entertainment in the city.

The verbal abuse reported by the refugees was mostly inflicted by groups of young people in their teens or early twenties. The students' reports of these incidents were characterized by such statements as 'They can spit on you when they pass in the street and call you names in front of everyone, you're embarrassed and ashamed' or 'on the street they call us thief because we're black.' This behaviour, which caused the refugee students considerable anxiety when they first came to Ireland, was reported to be a constant factor in students' lives and it has continued to be a cause of distress to them. They were all agreed that 'those who abused them did not differentiate between non-nationals on grounds of gender'. The female student in the group reported that, while stand-ing at a bus stop with a friend during the previous week, 'I was drenched with cold water by a man in a white van who called us f—ing blacks.' The male students agreed and said that 'They call our girls devils. They are bad to all foreigners – not so much to Europeans but to blacks, sometimes it's about religion.' The con-sensus among the group was that this form of name-calling, jostling and bullying was unpleasant, undermining, and a constant factor in their lives. However, it did not make them feel unsafe and it did not make them fear for their lives, as they had done before being granted asylum.

In the evenings and particularly after dark the refugees found their social situation to be more threatening than during the day. More long-standing refugees have warned them of the physical dangers that prevail in both the inner city and the city centre after nightfall. They recounted incidents in which foreigners were 'beaten up' or 'bumped off', and they all believed that the situation was much more dangerous for non-European foreigners. Notwithstanding this they believed that they were safer in Dublin in their home countries. If they were careful and stayed in at night they would be physically safe and they now had no need to fear 'a knock on the door in the middle of the night.' They also commented on the absence of 'real fear' for their families. One student said that he would not have to 'look at them killed in front of him now.'

The emotional impact of the abuse experienced by these refugees and on how they organized their lives was considerable. The terms 'exclusion' and 'isolated from Irish people' occurred in all the responses offered. They expressed a desire to be part of Irish life but they found it difficult to trust Irish people. One of the students seemed to sum up the feelings of the group. 'Some Irish are extremely friendly and make you feel relaxed but you can't relax because you don't know if they are making fun of you or not or setting you up.' They enjoy going to the cinema but avoid any social activities in the evenings and they believe that there are 'no clubs to join where you could do things like play football.' They like to walk in the city and visit the parks and they tend to spend their evenings watching television and studying. One refugee said his ambition was 'to get some place where I can spend my time and get integrated with the Irish', a sentiment which was echoed by the entire group.

Those members of the group who had travelled outside Dublin indicated a preference for living among the people of rural Ireland. One refugee suggested that 'the system of living in the countryside is not like Dublin, it is always difficult to live in a big city.' They suggested that the cause of much of the discrimination they experienced in Ireland was the pub culture, particularly among young people. They agreed that they are in the pubs too much, they drink and they smoke a terrible lot and anyway 'going to a pub for a night is a bad way to spend your time'. For some reason they had come to believe that 'it's the culture, because the Guinness was always made here in Dublin'. They also commented on the high cost of living in Dublin. They reported that their accommodation was very expensive and that when they have legal employment their wages 'vanish because everything is stopped out of their pay before they give it to you, and bills and rent take the rest and there is nothing left.' They all suggested that it was advisable to look-for private rented accommodation because 'council houses and flats were dangerous'. When pressed they admitted that they had no experience of this but that they had heard it from other refugees.

In spite of their reported isolation, of their experience of racist abuse and of a common antipathy to Irish weather, they declared they liked living in Ireland, and they believed that 'there were good and bad people here just like everywhere else'. They found their experience matched what they had been told to expect by other refugees and they believed that their lives would improve as 'the Irish got to know better that they were no harm'.

## Students' experience of dealing with the forces of the state, officialdom and their perspectives on the political system

There was general agreement among the group that discrimination by those in authority toward non-nationals, particularly to those who were not from the European Union was the norm. The comment 'you are always treated with suspicion, you always are made to wait and you are always made to feel small and ashamed' typifies their responses. This has engendered an atmosphere of insecurity and a feeling that their only security is in the avoidance of contact with officialdom in so far as this is possible. 'We do not always know our rights but if you go to ask it can mean trouble. Some people have been very good but we do not know who to trust.' This experience has resulted in the growth of informal net-works of non-nationals in which the more experienced refugees become the source of unofficial information about officialdom.

Every member of the group has experienced problems at airports and on the ferries. 'You are made to wait and wait like a criminal even when you have all the papers. In Dublin the guards can pick you up and if you don't have your papers you are in real big trouble.' One refugee reported being put in a cell for almost an hour because he had forgotten his papers. He considered this to be very unfair because he did have his bus pass and offered to go back to his home with the guards to get his papers. Another said that he had been taken off the ferry although he had an Irish passport. Travelling on the buses can be a problem for the refugees. One respondent said, 'some buses will pass the stop if there is only a black man there.' This was disputed by the remainder of the group who agreed 'the busmen were very good and helped them if other passengers caused trouble.' In general they were only mildly critical of the police and said they were 'not brutal' and they also commented that they 'were a whole lot better than the French ones'.

The refugees viewed the political system as generally good and more stable then those in their country of origin. The major advantage that they cited in this regard was their safety. 'Although they can do things to you in little ways, you will be safe and you won't be shot or something like that.' They did feel however that politicians were not sufficiently concerned about discrimination on grounds of race. 'A foreigner will never get a job if there is an Irish person in for it even if he is no good. They should have a law to stop this.' The same concern was voiced in relation to finding a flat or house to rent. They all believed that until discrimination is outlawed they could not be integrated into Irish society.

Their views on aspects of the Irish system of government and on political parties were somewhat complex. They read newspapers and watched news programmes on television, particularly if there was any discussion relevant to refugees. They were aware of the speech of the Minister for Justice, Equality and Law Reform, John O'Donoghue, at the launch of the Interdepartmental Working Group Report on the Integration of Refugees in Ireland in 2000. One student quoted his statement that he was 'committed to ensuring that all appropriate assistance is given to facilitate the integration into Irish society of those asylum seekers who are recognized as refugees or given leave to remain in the State on humanitarian grounds' almost *verbatim*. It was in the context of their acceptance of the existing political structures that they strongly expressed their views that more effective legislation should be enacted to deal with racial discrimination. They were not in favour of more liberal policies generally and they expressed admiration for Minister O'Donoghue and his policy of zero tolerance. They demonstrated an interest in political parties generally and although they expressed no particular political allegiance, some members were in favour of the policies of the Greens.

The Irish education system was considered by the group to be very good and they were generally happy with the educational provisions for refugees. They viewed the institution in which they were students very favourably and their views of their teachers were entirely positive. Their views on their fellow students from Ireland were less positive and more varied. Some refugees felt that Irish students tended to be impatient when their unfamiliarity with the language caused delay. This was viewed as indicative of a lack of understanding and sympathy for their position. The refugees also felt that their stated enthusiasm for achievement was viewed negatively by their Irish counterparts.

In general the members of the group were all interested in furthering their education so that they could have a good career and the rewards that this would bring. They reported spending a considerable amount of time on their studies, and all had plans for further progression. In general they felt that it would be through education that they would gain security for themselves and their families. They discussed various possible career paths. They were very interested in computing and IT and they were convinced that a career in this area would provide the rewards and stability to which they aspired. They mentioned a number of Irish celebrities who were 'black like ourselves.' They were proud of Paul McGrath and Phil Lynott who were from Dublin, and a number of other Irish footballers who had been born and brought up in the UK. However, they suggested that for this sort of success one had to be born in Ireland or the UK. As refugees they intended to take 'the slow but sure' road of 'hard study and keeping out of trouble'.

The purpose of this investigation was to ascertain the social and political learning needs of these students and to establish to what extent they found the existing provisions in this area accessible and relevant. It drew on the stories and the reported activities of the group with particular reference to their lives and experiences of social activities after school hours. In general the findings are indicative of a deficiency in the educational provision for the social and political learning needs of refugee students. Other findings highlight attitudinal problems in Irish society, indicative both of a lack of respect for the individual and a lack of tolerance and care for the integration of refugees into Irish society. Some of these hostile attitudes are evident in the manner in which some officials deal with refugees.

## Conclusions and recommendations

Some of the findings are indicative of an area of particular deficiency in educational provision for refugee students, while others highlight attitudinal problems in Irish society which are inimical to tolerance of refugees and their inclusion and integration into Irish society. The educational provision for refugees is viewed positively by refugees and it is considered adequate in terms of access, course availability and access to progression routes. What is lacking within the state provision is a Civic, Social and Political Education (CSPE) course or citizenship type programme tailored to meet the needs of refugee students. Consequently their access to information is at best haphazard and they are without the range of skills and information necessary to enter into the social life of the local community.

This lack of tolerance and hostile attitudes to refugees are evident in the manner in which some officials have been found to deal with non-nationals, particularly from non-European countries. This has resulted in distrust of the official methods of dealing with bureaucracy and the growth of informal support networks among the refugees themselves. Such networks may be helpful and can be instrumental in developing attitudes of self-reliance. However, they are not always reliable and may be based on anecdotal, irrelevant or erroneous information which, if acted upon, might increase the problems suffered by refugees. It seems desirable, therefore, that officials and representatives of the state who are responsible for dealing with refugees should be provided with in-service training. This would enable them to deal effectively and humanely with a situation which did not exist when many of them entered their particular service.

The discrimination suffered by refugee students as they went about their daily lives is the most serious finding of the study. This discrimination most usually took the form of verbal abuse and ridicule and less frequently physical abuse, which although reprehensible, was not perceived as life threatening. It seems likely that refugees in this age group are more vulnerable to this form of discrimination than either primary school pupils or adults. It is notable that the perpetrators of abuse were most usually of a similar age to the refugees. This seems to have had the effect of emphasizing the refugees' feelings of isolation from Irish society and specifically from their peers. This particular group have had little or no engagement with their Irish counterparts at a social level since they came to Ireland and they have been made to feel inadequate and demeaned. The CSPE programme for all Irish post-primary students must therefore find its context in the local community. Such issues as tolerance and respect for the individual must be approached not only on a theoretical level but within the communities in which students live.

The experiences of post-primary refugee students reported here are indicative of the failure to prevent the discrimination which has led to their social exclusion. This is in spite of the major efforts both at governmental level and within the voluntary sector in Ireland to provide educational opportunities for refugees, to prevent discrimination and to facilitate their integration. This would seem to indicate that a necessary ingredient is missing in current provisions. It seems likely that a more strategic approach to social and political education is required not only for refugees, but also for their fellow Irish students and for those officials who deal with refugees.

# 8

# Young people, citizenship and politics in Europe today

Hélène Feertchak

At a time when political analysts produce evidence of a whole series of changes that deeply affect the relationship between citizens and politics (Duchesne, 1997; Badie and Perrineau, 2000; Bréchon, 2000), psycho-sociologists may find it relevant to look at how politics and citizenship are perceived by young people.

How can we describe the new macro-political situation that characterizes the European states? How do these states differ in the way they address the issue of citizenship? Where does the young generation see itself? These questions are dealt with in the first part of this chapter. The second part focuses on the results of two complementary surveys of the perception of politics and citizenship of young French students aged between 18 and 25.

## Politics and citizenship: two core notions for Europeans

The evolution of democratic societies can be seen in many different ways: in the mode of political regulation, in how citizens evaluate the political supply, in citizens' behaviour, in the link between politics and territoriality, and in the uneasy co-existence of universalistic and particularistic values.

Of the many phenomena distinguishing current political life, five in particular have been examined by political analysts:

- the crisis of the State;

- challenging the political supply;

- the slump in traditional, indirect participation;

- confusion in the sense of territorial belonging; and

- the virtues of universalism versus those of particularism.

## The State in crisis

The State is traditionally perceived as linking power and legitimacy. A strong State deprived of legitimacy would be intolerable, while a wholly legitimate but impotent State would soon lose its ability to act. This apparent paradox underpins the authority of the State in democratic countries, although the proportions of legitimacy and power in each may vary because of national traditions (Lapierre, 2001).

In the case of France, the hegemony of the omnipresent 'Jacobin State' was well-tolerated during the '*Trente Glorieuses*' (The 'Thirty Glorious Years' of great economic growth between 1945 and 1975), as long as it firstly fully met its obligation of shielding the citizens from violence and threats (i.e. a 'regalian' type of State) and secondly was instrumental in equalizing social conditions (a 'redistributing' State). After this period the authority of the State was partially delegitimized: those who advocated '*moins d'État*' claimed the State concentrated too much power, while for others the State needed to reform itself to give more scope to actors at the local level. This defiance – which can be considered as the citizens' will to become free of the State – has recently been pushed back, as a strong demand for the State to protect has come forward. Mounting threats to social order (insecurity, terrorism, climatic hazards, environment, and food-related risks) lead to demands for the restoration of a protective State. The message currently being sent back to the State's representatives by citizens is a good example of paradoxical communication: we want more independence but we also demand more security.

## Challenging the political supply

Surveys carried out in various European states conclude that both politicians and political parties are suffering from a loss of credibility, and that this may be long-lasting. Public reaction to recent corruption scandals was more intense because politicians had also been seen to fail in their efforts to stamp out unemployment. The public was consistently being reminded that politicians had been elected 'to serve' rather than 'to serve themselves'. People now firmly believe that politicians pursue personal ambitions under the pretence of working for the public interest.

It has also been noted by political analysts that party proximity (that is, the interviewee's feelings of closeness to a political party) is declining and that the significance of the left–right divide is weakening as more people decline to place themselves on the left–right spectrum (Perrineau, 1996).

## The slump in traditional, indirect participation

Electoral participation in representative democracies – dropping one's ballot into the ballot box – is the traditional way for the citizen to partake in his or her country's political life. The extent of such participation is, however, decreasing throughout Europe (Topf, 1995; Perrineau, 1996), as the percentage of abstentions soars in many places. In France, for example, the abstention rate in the 1999 European Assembly poll was 53 per cent.

Two other types of behaviour are also increasing:

• *participation by protest*: activities such as signing petitions, boycotting products, demonstrating, staging sit-ins, and so on all aim to send direct messages to the authorities and bypass the elected representatives; and

• *participation by association*: citizens join forces to lobby and press to further their ideas, convictions and interests; here again, national elected representation is significantly bypassed.

While all political analysts link the decline of indirect participation to the increase in direct participation, they do not necessarily agree on how to extrapolate these trends and are not all equally optimistic as to how it might affect our long-term democratic life.

## The confusion of the sense of territorial belonging

Two forms of collective belonging are often associated in surveys: one is the sense of belonging to a well-defined geographical area, the other of belonging to a well-defined social class (Dirn, 1990; Bréchon, 2000). The clear trend in the case of France again goes back several decades (Dirn, 1990): the sense of belonging to a particular social class has tended to diminish, while sentiments of territorial belonging have become not so much national as infra-national (that is, related to the town or region) or supra-national (related to Europe, or even the world). In the third round of the *European Values Survey* (Bréchon, 2000, p. 69) the French answered the two questions concerning their territorial/social belonging with a high response rate. The answers showed a range of responses on a sense of geographical belonging, indicating that as 'Europe' comes into being, the population's potential spatial references are widening, with increased geographical mobility from professional factors and the democratisation brought about by foreign travel.

The individual citizen is faced with the choice of either clinging to his or her sentiment of national belonging (seen as psychologically essential) and accepting the increasing process of globalisation affecting our human existence or, on the other hand, he or she can protest against this evolution by insisting on the primacy of small-scale values.

Is the citizen of the world a 'unique' individual (as defined by Stirner), more unique than the citizen of the Nation State who might, in turn, be more unique than the citizen attached to the 'little motherland'? We cannot test this. What these responses indicate is that the interviewees, in their individual way, wish both to enjoy the autonomy of the modern subject and to feel part of a territory.

Some observers (Badie and Perrineau, 2000) stress that this 'deregulation' of the sense of belonging comes at a moment when globalisation seems apparently to be leading to a situation in which space is no longer an organizing principle of political life. Others suggest we should prioritise social systems, as opposed to political systems, and to networks rather than hierarchies, thus turning one's back on territorial encasing and the very notion of the territorial State. Should we go so far as to say, along with Jean-William Lapierre (2001), that 'We must consider de-territorializing the political realm'?

## The virtues of universalism versus those of particularism

This debate has now opened, stemming from the competition between the French republican pattern – born of the French Revolution – in which the concept of *equality* prevails, and the Anglo-Saxon democratic pattern in which the concept of *freedom* is paramount. The universalistic, reputedly modern, values that used to prevail in Europe over the particularistic values, hitherto seen as overly tied to the past, have suffered badly from several factors; these include a sense of community which is developing in all areas (ethnic, religious, etc.), the challenging of neutrality (a term used in Germany) and of secularity (as used in France in the word '*laïcité*'), and the lobbying practices imported from the United States and currently used in the European institutions (Badie and Perrineau, 2000).

The fragile equilibrium once achieved between the individual and the collective fields is in danger from the pressure of various identities, each now calling for recognition in the Hegelian sense of the word.

## Analysis

Political analysts are often asked whether, in view of these changes in the relationship between citizens and politics, it is necessary to link them to broader theories on the evolution of western societies. Their responses are always cautious: attractive though it sounds, demonstrating a causal relationship between citizens' feelings of increased scepticism and their escalating individualism is rather difficult to prove.

With caution in mind, it may usefully be pointed out that although the concept of a new era, usually designated with a 'post' prefix has allegedly begun, another line of reasoning is possible, that suggests the phenomena are cyclical.

Daniel Bell (1973, 1976) suggests cultural changes in post-industrial societies have led to capitalism losing its coherence. Change for change's sake – when revolt becomes conformism – inevitably leads to uniformity, and the extension of hedonism leads to individual pleasure-seeking becoming the core of post-modern culture, a culture that turns its back on Protestant ethics and on the obligation to save before consuming. Christopher Lasch (1979) famously used the image of Narcissus to symbolise the new individual: a self-obsessed person, hyperconscious about his or her looks, who wishes to be envied rather than respected. Narcissus deserts politics and loses 'all sense of historical continuity': indifferent to the future and viewing the past as devalued, he is no longer aware of the passing of generations. Richard Sennett (1974) denounces what he sees as the soft tyranny that lies under the cover of apparently benevolent authenticity: today's individual, despite his or her genuine willingness to appear sincere and transparent, can no longer respect others because they can no longer play the social roles that once existed. Gilles Lipovetsky (1983) has introduced the public in France to the theses of these American authors, at the same time criticising their liking for catastrophes on the one hand, and their neo-puritanism on the other.

Ronald Inglehart (1977, 1990, 1997) is more optimistic: proposing the idea of post-materialistic values derived from the views of the psychologist Maslow. He argues that materialistic values have lost out to post-materialistic values such as freedom of expression and partaking in decision-making, because more recent generations have, during their youth, not been preoccupied by material survival.

131

All these visions make a sharp contrast between a 'beforehand' that will never return and an 'afterwards': let us as a counterpoint recall the analysis of Alfred Hirschman (1982), a great reader of Vico (Hirschman, 1977). For him, societies follow a cyclical pattern in which people alternately engage in public life and then focus on the self-centered pursuit of their private happiness. Each of these phases starts in a satisfactory manner, but then disappointment sets in – hence the reversal.

Within this plethora of ideas and oft-cited theories, we can see the wide choice available to the political analyst to describe political changes in the global context.

## Differences between countries

### Politics
Political scientists have long been aware of the wide variance in the degree of politicisation shown in different European states: the French for instance have for many decades not shown as much interest in politics as their European neighbours (Bréchon, 2000). Recent data published in the *Eurobarometers* show that there are, however, fewer un-politicised citizens in Europe: but in France the percentage remains stable, but high (see also Edye in Chapter 6). The latest *European Values Surveys* (EVS) survey shows that 35 per cent of the French population never talk about politics with their friends (see also Kerkhofs in Chapter 10). The French have a unique attitude towards politics: Jean-Pierre Rosanvallon's analysis (1992) concludes 'France characterizes itself by the great difficulty it has conceptualising the political field.' Legislative power is traditionally held in higher esteem than executive power – more often than not dismissed as the mere managing of tasks – and this makes the task of defining the political field more difficult. The French find it particularly problematic to have 'great principles' co-existing with 'small, discreet arrangements'.

Specialists in constitutional law suggest that this inhibition goes back to the 1789 Declaration of the Rights of Man: 'By opposing the notions of arbitrariness and lawfulness, Article 7 expresses in a concrete way a sense of defiance towards the questionable executive power and its trust in an intrinsically liberating legislative power' (Morabito and Bourmaud, 1993). Faced with a choice between man and citizen, the drafters of the Declaration unwaveringly chose to favour the citizen – he who votes and contributes, through his representatives, to the making of the law – as an expression of the general will.

Apart from this faith in the legislative process, so characteristic of France as opposed to the Anglo-Saxon world, there is another noteworthy difference: the distinction between the general interest and the specific interest (Rosanvallon, 1992). French political tradition has it that the former, associated with rationality and truth, cannot be inferred from the latter, which is linked to a narrowness of vision: it is simply impossible to shift from one to the other by mere construction. The English tradition, of a very different empirical nature, is said by Rosanvallon to see the general interest as a 'mere compound' of all the specific interests.

## Citizenship

Citizenship is a fashionable and at times banal concept, which is also a legal term that is often seen as vague (Lochak, 1991). It is a daunting concept to study cross-culturally, particularly within the European framework. 'Citizen' has different meanings in different countries, which creates a logical difficulty: should we distinguish citizens from two countries as having different conceptions of citizenship, or should we consider that their differences simply stem from the respective languages which they use to describe the concept? In other words, we are requiring a linguistic tool to answer a question that is dependant on that very tool; this is what the logician Carnap called the 'self-predictable character' of certain concepts.

Analysts often compare the French case to that of Germany, for three reasons:

- the historical opposition between two sets of traditions – the right of blood in Germany, and the right of the soil in France. The recent *Bundesrat* Act implementing the right of the soil in Germany which came into force in 2000 is a genuine historical turning point (Kastoryano, 2000);

- the co-existence of the two Germanys which gave rise, over half a century, to a heated debate on the distinction between nationality and citizenship; and

- the two different terms in the German language: *Stadtsbürger* (townsman ship) and *Staatsbürger* (citizenship). Citizenship which applies to the municipal realm cannot, for historical reasons, be confused with national citizenship (Rosanvallon, 1992).

The variations shown in the *Eurobarometer* surveys reflect the difficulty of studying citizenship in several European countries as it is experienced. In one question the interviewees were asked whether or not they felt European as well as French (or German, Italian, etc.): interestingly, the wording of the question varied, the word 'citizen' appearing and disappearing from year to year (Duchesne, 1997). Duchesne suggests it may not be possible to study citizenship in a uniform way in different European countries, as evocations vary from one country to another and from population to population. Indeed, 'It seems that the words '*Bürger*' and '*cittadino*' did not convey anything concrete to them, but that they were typical of administrative vocabulary'. This is not the case in France, where the word has a very emotional undertone. Alfred Grosser emphasizes the 'sentimentality of the French Revolution [which] maintained itself through the word "citizen" ' (Grosser, 2000).

Duchesne also stresses the particularity of the French situation, in that citizenship cannot be envisaged other than through its link to the national community, which is not the case in other European countries or in the United States. This French specificity comes from the Revolutionary period; the experience of a natural link with the nation dates from that period, and replaces the older attachments to such natural communities as family, religion, corporation or region. The two patterns of citizenship developed – 'of inheritance' and 'of scruples' – are opposed: the former focuses on the assimilative nature of citizenship and nationality, and on the role played by the family in the transmission of values, while the latter focuses on inter-individual relations and social life. However, both share the notion that the citizen has duties: he or she must either contribute to increasing the joint patrimony or must work, participating in the life of the city, to earn the advantages bestowed upon him or her.

The originality of this 'citizenship *à la française*' lies in the tension between these two patterns. This social representation allows all citizens to navigate between these two poles that are theoretically opposed, prioritising duties or rights, permanence or change, particularism or universalism. If the nation is seen as the sole basis of citizenship, this allows both the cohesion and the inclusion of individuals, alternately referring to themselves as 'us' or 'I'. The *a priori* antinomic character of our holistic and individualistic visions of belonging disappears, as everyone can pass from one pattern to the other through themes such as the vote, seen as the prototype of one's right and duty.

### Age-related variations

The French situation is different from the Anglo-Saxon world in terms of politics and from Germany in terms of citizenship: this chapter will now focus on France in this study of young people's views in the surveys.

The regular surveys carried out by the polling organization SOFRES show that the drop in public interest in politics over the past twenty years (from 60 per cent to about 45 per cent) has been moderated by socio-cultural variables and by the age factor: the proportion of young people aged between 18 and 24 who are interested in politics is as low as 36 per cent (Méchet and Weill, in Badie and Perrineau, 2000).

The EVS surveys confirm this trend (Bréchon, 2000, p. 107): in 1999 46 per cent of the interviewees in the 18 to 26 years bracket (compared to only 39 per cent in 1990) said they never talked about politics with their friends. This is a generation-related shift: today's younger generation is generally speaking less politicised than the earlier age band.

Another phenomenon emphasized by Bréchon is the effect of politicisation on the electoral participation rate: this is lowest among the young as shown by the 1999 figures when the potential abstention rate in the 18 to 29 year bracket was three times greater among the less politicised than among the highly politicised. It was only two times greater amongst those aged 60 years and over. The category corresponding to the oldest voters shows a weaker link between politicisation and participation: it is not unusual for them to vote even if they have a total lack interest in politics (Bréchon, 2000, p. 112).

Beyond these age-related differences, it can be seen that education has a greater effect within the youngest generation of voters. A CEVIPOF (*Centre d'étude de la vie politique française*) survey carried out recently by the Home Ministry's *Centre d'Etude et de Prévision* indicates that the lack of interest in politics shown by young people living in 'underprivileged' areas stems from a sense of incompetence: they feel outwitted by practices and discourse that they cannot decipher, have only a vague knowledge of the actors and institutions, and have been ill-prepared for political socialization by their families. The awareness of the significance of the act of voting is closely correlated to their level of schooling.

## Citizenship

Duchesne's research shows that age is the variable which most affects what people have to say in interview: the interviewees who fit into the inheritance pattern are on average older (55 years) than those listed in the scruples pattern (37 years). Duchesne discusses the implications of this by analysing this in relation to period, generation and age (Duchesne, 1997, p. 313 *et seq.*).

This period-related effect might be an irreversible trend, charac-teristic of post-industrial society, in which the centre of gravity of the process is shifting towards greater individualism, but with some degree of inertia, particularly amongst older people.

If we are dealing here with a generation-related effect, then the scruples pattern corresponds to the generation who were young during the '*Trente Glorieuses*' (see *supra*), and it is difficult to predict how it will evolve beyond a period of more than a few decades.

If it is an age-related effect, then an individual will, at different stages in his or her life, favour group identification or awareness of full-fledged human being, this pattern of alternation being a mani-festation of human adaptability. This might be in keeping with the argument that mental representations have an adaptive value for the individual, who must consider the changing situations he meets and his interactions with an 'other' who is also endowed with his or her own mental representations (Lahlou, 1998).

## Politics and citizenship: survey results

The two surveys dealt with here were conducted in 2000 and 2001. The young interviewees were 75 per cent female and 25 per cent male, aged between 18 and 25 years, and all were Arts or Social Sciences students in the Greater Paris area. The sex variable was not taken into account when constituting the panel and was simply recorded: it did not introduce any notable difference.

The questionnaire was very short, consisting of two closed questions followed by an open one: there were two near identical versions. The interviews were carried out in collective sessions in each venue. The students received one or the other version, but were not aware of this, as the page appearance was very similar.

The first closed question dealt with the individual's sense of terri-torial belonging and the second with their political self-positioning on a left to right scale. The open question addressed either the associations brought about by the stimulus word *Politics* or those brought about by the word *Citizenship* as follows: 'Can you say what politics mean to you?' or 'Can you say what it means to you to be a citizen?'

The question on the sense of territorial allegiance or belonging was for one of the questionnaires taken from the EVS Survey question-naire (Bréchon, 2000), and for the other from the CEVIPOF questionnaire (Boy, Mayer, 1997). The former put forward five territorial levels – town, region, country, Europe and the world – encased one within the other. The other questionnaire was different: respondents were asked to compare their sense of national and European belonging on a five-point scale (feeling 'only French', 'more French than European', 'as French as European', 'more European than French' or 'only European').

The question on self-positioning on a left–right scale was also borrowed either from the EVS questionnaire, which had a ten-point scale, or from the CEVIPOF one, which had a seven-point grading system.

Results were collected from 78 respondents for Version 1 (the EVS survey wording, and stimulus word Politics), and from 62 respon-dents for Version 2 (the CEVIPOF wording and stimulus-word Citizenship).

Comparison of the political position on the left–right scale showed that the two scales used gave almost identical distributions: after re-coding of the grades to a common scale, about half the inter-viewees positioned themselves on the left, one third in the centre and one tenth on the right.

The relationship between territorial allegiance and of political positioning was found to be dependant on the wording used in the first question:

* When the encased list of items was used, there was a clear relationship: those who aligned themselves as left preferred supra-national references to Europe or World (42 per cent) to infra-national references to town or region (17%). Conversely,

those who defined themselves as on the right only preferred the supra-national references in 20 per cent of cases, compared to 40 per cent selecting infra-national choices.

• When the second questionnaire was used, which only offered a simple comparison between national and European belonging, there was no connection between the two. This can be explained as a consequence of the way the question forces a polarity on the respondents.

The responses to the open-ended questions on citizenship and politics were subjected to content analysis, and then cross-tabulated with the responses to the closed questions, and these were then factor analysed.

## Politics

The content analysis of the answers given to the open question 'Can you say what politics mean to you?' gave three dimensions: one attitude-related (*Attitude*) and two cognitive (*Actors* and *Facets*). The interviewees clearly held extremely varied views, covering a wide spectrum, but could be divided into two similar sized groups, half expressing a broadly favourable attitude towards politics and half an unfavourable or indifferent attitude.

Political *Actors* are mentioned in under one third of all answers, with no particular focus. The responses in the *Facets* dimension (Table 1) also show a variety of perspectives on issues of political supply, which are grouped under four categories (*Corruption*, *Lies*, *Inattentiveness*, *Power Struggles*) and mentioned by about three-quarters of all respondents.

The initial examination of the variations in codings examined the cognitive richness of the answers. A pointer was established as the *sum total of mentions of Actors + sum total of mentions of Facets* (averaging 2.99). This varied according to attitude and political positioning but not to the sense of territorial belonging.

| Table 1: Content analysis of responses to Politics: Cognitive dimension Facets (percentage of 78 responses) | | |
|---|---|---|
| Category | Typical responses | % |
| Institutions | functioning, system, management | 49 |
| Debates | Divergent opinions, expressing oneself | 26 |
| power struggles | hitting at each other, competition, conflict | 23 |
| Corruption | sleaze, trickery, underhand operations, scandals | 21 |
| Lies | unkept promises, deceitful speeches, hypocrisy | 21 |
| Ideologies | ideas, ideals, ideologies, utopias | 17 |
| Inattentiveness | far from people's everyday concerns | 13 |
| Inaccessibility | reserved for the elite, ENA,[1] barriers | 8 |
| Fear of the National | Front worrying, must vote against | 4 |
| Confused responses | complicated, complex, vague | 17 |

**Attitude**

| favourable | indifferent | unfavourable |
|---|---|---|
| 3.41 | 2.20 | 2.69 |

**Political positioning**

| Right | Centre | Left | extreme Left |
|---|---|---|---|
| 3.4 | 2.65 | 2.70 | 3.31 |

It would seem that young citizens who self-positioned themselves on the extremes of the political spectrum have the most argumentative political vision, despite their divergent opinions.

This can be checked by comparing this attitude with political positioning: the *Attitude* coded as *Critical but hopeful* is found more frequent in the extreme-left category (31 per cent, only 17 per cent on the right), while the *Attitude* coded as *Keen* is found more amongst the right (40 per cent, compared to only 15 per cent on the extreme left). The variations of the cognitive dimensions (*Actors* and *Facets*) under the effect of the political positioning are as follows:

- young people on the extreme left, more often than any other category, fear the *National Front*, mention *Citizens*, the *Inattentiveness* of political actors and the presence of *Ideology*;

- those in the centre most frequently refer to *Institutions*; and

- those on the right most often mention *Country* and *Debates*.

The themes related to *Corruption* and *Power Struggles* do not vary according to political position.

The relationship between these dimensions and the sense of territorial belonging shows a strong contrast between those young people who have infra-national identifications (to town or region) and those who show supra-national identification (to Europe or the world):

- the infra-national group more frequently show a *Keen* attitude, and mention *Country*, *town*, *institutions* or *ideologies*;

- the supra-national group more often say they feel *Excluded* from politics, or that they are *Critical but hopeful*, that they conceive politics as being aware of the *Citizens* and that they perceive politicians as *inattentive* and politics to be *inaccessible* or *confused*.

The correlations between the dimensions that were established in the content analysis show a strong relationship between the attitudinal dimension (*Attitude* to politics) and the two cognitive ones (*Actors* and *Facets*).

- interviewees expressing an *Unfavourable* attitude to politics refer to *Town* or *Country* in 11 per cent of cases, while those to expressing a *Favourable* attitude refer to these in 33 per cent of cases;

- interviewees expressing an *Unfavourable* attitude to politics most frequently refer to *Corruption, Lies, Inattentive* political staff and *Inaccessible* politics, while those to expressing a *Favourable* attitude mention *Debates*, the *Institutions* and the *Ideological Supply* most often.

Cross-tabulating all the *Facets* categories gives two sets of answers, about politics *as it is* and those about politics *as it should be*:

- Politics as it is: these young people connect *Corruption* and *Lies*, with a frequency of the *Corruption* coding of 14 per cent of the 231 codings, rising to 38 per cent when the answer also refers to *Lie*;

- Politics as it should be: these connect *Debates, Institutions* and *Ideology*: the *Debates* category yields a 15 per cent frequency of codings but rising to 30 per cent when the answer also refers to *Institutions*, and to 26 per cent when it also refers to *Ideology*.

Factorial analysis confirms the logical structure underpinning the very different representation of politics shown by these young people, who are of the same age and have comparable levels of education. The most interesting sub-group is of those who appear to go against the tendency towards scepticism *vis-à-vis* politics: they insist on connecting politics to a territory – country or town – and on seeing politics as institutions that go beyond mere management, and focus on intellectual debate based on grand principles and ideals. These *Keen* young people are to be found more frequently on the right, but also on the extreme left of the political spectrum.

## Citizenship

The content analysis of the answers given to the open question on citizenship revealed two cognitive dimensions. The distinction between these two category systems was made on a grammatical basis. The first table is of the verbs used by the interviewees (Table 2) and the second table is of the concepts mentioned as nouns (Table 3).

**Table 2: Content analysis of responses to Citizenship: Cognitive dimension based on Verbs (percentage of 62 responses; multiple responses)**

| Major category | Percentage | Subcategory | Percentage |
|---|---|---|---|
| To participate, to vote | 71 | to participate | 58 |
| | | to vote | 50 |
| | | to contest | 3 |
| To respect | 65 | to respect | 52 |
| | | to have | 26 |
| To belong | 47 | to be part of | 32 |
| | | to feel | 19 |
| | | to be recognized | 5 |
| | | to love | 2 |
| To live with | 37 | to live with | 21 |
| | | to help | 11 |
| | | to share | 7 |
| | | Not to harm | 3 |
| To be interested in | 16 | to be interested | 10 |
| | | to know | 8 |

The categories are clearly defined and show how the interviewees develop several ideas in each of their answers: there are approximately five items for each respondent. The analysis of these against the respondents' political positioning shows sharp variations in the table of *Verbs* and in table of *Nouns*.

The respondents were recoded as to their expressed territorial identification. Those who responded that they felt 'only French' or 'more French than European' (about 50 per cent) were categorised as '*Nationalists*', while those who felt 'as French as European', 'more European than French' and 'only European' (about 25 per cent) were grouped under the heading '*Europeanist*'. The remaining quarter did not wish to position themselves.

**Table 3: Content analysis of responses to Citizenship:
Cognitive dimension based on Nouns
(percentage of 62 responses; multiple responses)**

| Major category | Percentage | Subcategory | Percentage |
|---|---|---|---|
| Rights and duties | 65 | rights and duties | 27 |
| | | duties (only) | 8 |
| | | rights (only) | 3 |
| | | laws and regulations | 37 |
| | | ideals and values | 7 |
| Others | 57 | community | 40 |
| | | others | 29 |
| Territory | 55 | national territory | 53 |
| | | local territory | 8 |
| | | European territory | 2 |
| | | world territory | 2 |
| Common destiny | 31 | political, economic, social | 24 |
| | | History, culture, language, tradition | 13 |
| Democracy | 26 | Opinion | 13 |
| Freedom | 10 | Institutions | 8 |
| | | Democracy | 5 |

| Verb: | | left | right |
|---|---|---|---|
| | To belong | 16 | 29 |
| | To participate/to vote | 33 | 24 |

| Noun: | | left | right |
|---|---|---|---|
| | Territory | 19 | 32 |
| | Democracy | 16 | 4 |

These two variations are very closely interconnected, indicating two core meanings, each expressed by a Verb/Noun couplet: *To belong to/Territory* and *To vote/Democracy*.

The analysis of territorial belonging when re-coded in this way demonstrates a number of differences in how *Nationalists* and *Europeanists* act. The *Nationalists* more frequently use verbs such as *To participate* or *To vote* (35 per cent), which are less used by the *Europeanists* (21 per cent). Conversely, *Europeanists* are more likely to use expressions such as *To be interested in* (11 per cent) that the *Nationalists* (5 per cent).

Examining the categories used in the cognitive dimension based on nouns (Table 3), there are again differences between the two.

- the *Nationalists* more frequently refer to *Others*, whether in the form of *Others* or of *Community*, and *Political, Economic and Social* problems are more frequently mentioned;

- the *Europeanists* more often refer to *History, culture, language, traditions* and mention more often *Laws and regulations* and *Institutions*.

This rather more scholarly response of the *Europeanists'* answers is confirmed by the richness of their responses: they give an average of 5.3 responses of verbs and nouns, as against only 4.6 by the *Nationalists*. Factor analysis shows a close relationship between the *Europeanists* and the verb *To be interested,* and between the interviewees who are self-positioned on the left and *Democracy*. It also suggests a conflict between the expertise of those who are *Interested* and the sentimentalism of those who consider they are citizens insofar as they are primarily fellow-citizens. Possession of Duties and Rights, and respect for these same Duties and Rights, appear to be a centre of gravity for ideas such as sentiment, expertise and participation. All of these give access to the representation that finds its coherence in a I/Others characteristic of citizenship.

## Conclusion

Comparing the results from the use of the two stimulus words *Politics* and *Citizenship* leads to several conclusions. Firstly, the idea of **citizenship** is disconnected from the sphere of politics, which is burdened with disparaging associations. The citizen is a person who lives among other persons, and the ideas of either a shared territory or interpersonal relationships are stressed. The smooth transition between these various representations accords with Duchesne's results, and also suggests the 'learnt' (as in learnt by heart at school) character of this very abstract concept.

Secondly, it should be noted that these interviewees had a higher level of schooling than average; and it may not be possible to extrapolate from these findings when dealing with young people less accustomed to abstract reasoning. Less educated young people might need concrete anchoring and have difficulty in seeing themselves as both 'I' and 'Us'.

Finally, there was a particular conception of **politics** developed by a small number of interviewees, identified as the 'keen' group. In their eyes, politics corresponds to a space for public communication, where exchanges and words are paramount: this is close to Habermas' conception (1981). When other interviewees might appear to be more critical, this was because of the perversity of political discourse, with so many accusations that politicians' speeches are deceitful and misleading. Worse, politicians are seen to speak but not to listen. Analysis of the exchange between politicians and ordinary citizens is ridded with difficulty.

These considerations may be of use to those interested in promoting the idea of Europe. The question of how a twenty-year-old can believe in Europe at the beginning of the twenty-first century is fundamental, but it may mask an equally key question: how can today' twenty-year-old believe in politics?

## Note

1.   ENA: '*Ecole Nationale d'Administration*', a '*grande école*' where top-level bureaucrats are trained.

# 9

# The introduction of the euro as a means to create a new feeling of territorial belonging

Christine Roland-Lévy

What do children and young people understand about their political environment? Does their way of understanding develop in the same order – as suggested by Piaget – when the social, economic and political contexts are changing? These are fundamental questions for educators. This chapter aims to show the effects on political socialisation of the changes in the social, economic and political environment brought about by the switch to the euro. Socialisation refers to the process of maturation as a child learns to comprehend the world of adults. Political socialisation specifically refers to the process by which a child develops an understanding of the world of politics. This is related to 'naive politics', or politics perceived by non-specialists. Even though teenagers are 'naive' subjects, they are familiar with some aspects of the political world, and possess some knowledge and understanding of how it works, as much as do many adults. Theories and methodological techniques used in research on socialisation, especially in economic socialization, are considered in Roland-Lévy (1998, 2000, 2002 a).

This chapter uses two series of studies to analyse the effect of the introduction of the euro-currency on young people's perception of Europe. It is suggested that the feeling of 'belonging to Europe', along with the impression of 'being a European' has changed with the simultaneous introduction of the common European currency in the twelve countries of the euro-zone. It is hypothesised that this perception depends on certain psychological variables, related to both the subjects themselves and to their degree of familiarity with the euro. Attitudes toward the euro and its social representations are compared, six months before its introduction and during the months of January and February 2002 when the euro became the single currency. Two different samples of teenage subjects were studied and compared in each of these two periods. Data on the influence of the euro on one's feeling of becoming more European are discussed.

## Territorial belonging: national or European

The main purpose of the project was to explore national identity, with the feeling of belonging, compared to European identity. Europe has now reached a concrete stage in the process of European integration, with the introduction of a single currency. Recent research has addressed issues around monetary integration. An earlier study (Müller-Peters et al., 1998) demonstrated that in most countries attitudes toward the euro are positively correlated with attitudes toward the European Union. Pepermans and Verleye (1998) showed that the latter are also linked to perceptions of national features. The results obtained by van Everdingen and van Raaij (1998) also specify that national identity has indirect effects on attitudes, by influencing expectations about the euro. Meier and Kirchler (1998) reported that opponents, indifferent respondents and supporters of the euro, are distinguished on the basis of social representations, which vary in content and structure. More importantly, the difference between opponents and supporters refers to national preoccupations about identity, which are linked to the feeling of territorial belonging.

In various previous studies (some of which are referred to by Feertchak in Chapter 8), it is clear that in France the former sense of belonging – which used to be rooted in social class – is now clearly evolving towards a new feeling of territorial belonging (Dirn,

1990). A specific analysis of the latest *European Values Survey* by Bréchon (2000) found that, in 1999, the feeling of belonging seemed to be evolving towards territorial belonging, either national and/or infra national (83 per cent of respondents selecting 'town, region, or country'), or a supranational (15 per cent select 'Europe, the world') feeling of belonging. The individual is now faced with the choice of having either a local territorial belonging, or a more global belonging. Compared to previous EVS, the answers to the question on geographical belonging indicate that, as Europe comes into being, its population's potential spatial references are widening as geographical mobility develops because of professional factors and the democratisation of increased travel abroad. Even so, results in 1999 showed that only 4 per cent selected Europe as their personal choice in terms of belonging. This chapter explores the feeling of national versus European belonging among teenagers that are raised by the introduction of the euro, drawing on these recent analyses.

## Attitudes and social representations

Social representations express the values, norms and attitudes of social groups, and this therefore allows the analysis of how a new object, the euro, was perceived both while it was still virtual and once it became a reality. Because the representation of a social object is a description of how it is perceived, there should be a strong relationship between the social representation of this object and the subject's attitude toward it. This study aims at showing how a new representation is gradually built, from different individual attitudes, and is shared by many, thus becoming, little by little, a shared social representation. The analysis of a sample of teenagers should bring more information on how social representations are being constructed. It is particularly interesting to study the general attitude toward the euro among our samples, the goal being, on the one hand, to examine the relations between social representations and attitudes, and on the other hand, to study potential links between them and national versus European identity.

Initially conceived by Durkheim (1898) at the end of the nineteenth century, the concept of social representation was revived by Moscovici (1961, 1989) in his study of psychoanalysis in French society. Social representations are social forms of knowledge, free from scientific constraints and formalized in figurative *schemata*. They can serve as a basis for perceiving and interpreting reality, as well as for channelling people's behaviour. Furthermore, they are related to the social characteristics of people. Empirical evidence shows that it is often possible to distinguish different social representations corresponding to particular social groups. Moscovici's initial formulation focused on the genesis of social representations through two major processes. Objectivation first translates some of the characteristics of an unfamiliar object, such as a new currency, into the terms of our realities. The different stages involved in this process include the selection of information, decontextualization and reconstruction into a schema, built with certain dimensions. Anchoring includes two different aspects: a cognitive aspect in which the object is integrated into the previous thoughts of individuals (e.g. the euro perceived as a currency in the same way as the French franc); the second aspect is a social one, having to do with a social group giving meaning to a representation; for example, a meaning of an awareness of Europe. Thus, interpretations of a particular object differ from one social group to another.

Since Moscovici's early work, different theoretical approaches have been developed. One of these considers the cognitive organisation of social representations in terms of different kinds of elements, central versus peripheral. According to Abric's (1976, 1994) structural approach, social representations are composed of a central nucleus surrounded by peripheral elements. This theoretical approach, based on a hierarchical structure of the representation, can be complemented by Flament's (1962, 1981), which deals with specific internal structure of the representation. This chapter refers to both theories, using two different methodological approaches. A variety of techniques should be used to study social representations; here, two techniques are used to study the social representations of the new currency. The first is based on tasks of free association, and the second on the selection of blocks of items that form the core of the representation.

A comparison of the feeling of belonging to one's own country (France) with the feeling of being European is explored, in relation to knowledge about the European Union and about the European Monetary Union, linked with attitudes to and with representations of the euro.

## Method

This chapter analyses attitudes and social representations of the euro, both six months before its introduction and during early 2002, when the euro became the common currency. It was hypothesised that differences would be found in terms of social representations and attitudes, before and after the arrival of the euro. The feeling of belonging might also change from phase one to phase two as a concrete single European currency came to be used. Two samples of teenagers were studied to test this during these two distinct periods. A questionnaire was designed to investigate attitudes toward the national currency and the euro, and social representations, along with the feeling of belonging. In this questionnaire, subjects' representations related mainly to the euro were considered first. A series of attitude scales were designed to measure the attitudes toward the euro and Europe. Subjects were also asked to identify the various countries belonging to the European Monetary Union. With the practical use of the new single currency, both social representations and attitudes were expected to change between the two phases, before and after the introduction of the euro. These changes are likely to have an impact on the feeling of belonging to Europe itself.

### Population and samples for the two phases of the study

In the first phase, a small sample of 52 French teenagers (age 14 to 18, mean 15.6) was selected from Paris and its suburban area. Equal number of girls and boys, from different social backgrounds and with a large variety of types and levels of education, were interviewed during this first phase with a face-to-face questionnaire.

In the second phase, 205 French young people from varied social backgrounds were chosen; this sample was composed of 107 teenage girls and 98 boys (aged 11 to 18, mean 14.5). The teenagers for the second phase were interviewed between the second week of January and the second week of February 2002.

## Material and procedures

Because the euro currency was virtual in phase one and real in phase two, a different technique was used to study its social representations for each phase.

In phase one, subjects' representations of the upcoming currency were tested according to Abric's central core hypothesis (1976, 1982, 1984, 1988), based on free association tasks. Vergès' methodological tools were used to investigate the composition of the central nucleus of social representations (1992, 1998, 2001), both in terms of frequency and of rank of appearance of the evoked terms. According to this theory, most subjects express the terms belonging to the shared nucleus; they will be spontaneously produced by many subjects (high frequency); and as these terms are important to the group, they will also be among those first called to mind (which is referred to as having a low ranking). Conversely, the periphery, which takes into account individuality, categorizes terms which are not shared by many people, and therefore which have a low frequency; the peripheral elements usually occur later in terms of recall, with at a high rank. The combination of frequency and rank shows the position of representation in the hierarchy.

In phase two, subjects' representations of the euro and of the French franc were compared, with an analysis of the connections between them (cf. Flament, 1962, 1981; Degenne and Vergès, 1973; Degenne, 1985; Vergès, 1985); the aim of this technique is to explore how terms are related to each other, thus revealing the internal structure of the representation. Based on an adaptation of Guimelli's methodological tool, founded on the selection of blocks of items (1989), each subject was presented with a list of 25 items chosen from the list of words which had been produced in the first phase. Respondents were asked to select the five items they felt best represented the euro, and the five they considered least representative of the euro; the remaining 15 items were considered neutral. The same procedure was adopted for the French franc. With this technique, which is an alternative way of identifying the structure of the representation, one can identify terms that are strongly linked with connection a score, which can also be represented graphically using the Kruskal algorithm to produce Kruskal trees, which show the links between items.

In both phases, subjects were also asked to rank a series of nine Likert-type attitude scales related to the new currency. After factor analysis, all nine scales were kept, as each proved to be reliable ($\alpha$ = .6590). Combined together, the scales generate an attitudinal score that defines the general attitude of the subjects toward the euro (from positive scores of between 3 to 5, and negative scores from 0 to 2).

In order to test whether our subjects felt they were French rather than European, or European rather than French, a specific direct open-ended question was asked: '*Do you feel European? Explain how and why*'. Content analysis was used to categorise the types of response. To test their familiarity with Europe, a list of 20 countries – the 12 countries of the European Monetary Union with other European countries and countries such as Israel and Turkey – was presented to subjects: they were asked to identify which countries belonged to the euro-zone. Personal characteristics such as age, gender and schooling were also recorded. Subjects took approximately half an hour to complete the questionnaire.

## Results
Representations, attitudes and feeling of belonging were compared for the phases of before and after January 2002. Results are

presented for the two samples of subjects identifying appropriate gender differences.

## Similarities and divergence of representations

The comparison representations based on the virtual practice of the euro, and then on the concrete daily use of notes and coins showed the following.

In the first phase the 52 teenagers express clear distinctions between the French franc and the euro. For all of the subjects, the franc was the shared symbol of *France*; this emblem was made the centre of the representation by the fact that it is *money*. Two-thirds of the sample mention *notes and coins* in the near periphery. The franc is also linked to *spending,* which is also in the near periphery.

*Europe* is the most central element of the social representation of the euro, but it is undoubtedly *money* for two-thirds of the subjects. Other terms which appear in the near periphery – and could easily slide to the centre – of the euro representation include the notion of *union,* which is produced by the majority of teenagers with a low rank. Teenagers also include *novelty* in the centre of their repre-sentation; *complexity* is also central, and is often linked to the diffi-culties of *conversions.* Against this, they consider that life will be easier with a *single currency* throughout the euro-zone, and that it will definitely facilitate international *exchanges*; both of these ideas appear in the periphery of their representation of the euro.

The franc and the euro appear to symbolize different objects – the different territories of France and Europe – but the social repre-sentations of both items can be clearly linked to the concept of *money* through selection of information, decontextualization and later reconstruction.

In the phase after the euro was introduced, the euro is still obviously perceived as the symbol of *Europe* on examining the terms which were most often chosen from the list of 25 possible items. The group of teenagers tends at this moment to have a shared representation of the euro focused around four key notions: *Europe, union, novelty* and *money*. Of the main items selected as symbols to contrast with the euro, the *Dollar* comes first, followed by *complexity* and – surprisingly – *easiness*. Nothing has changed in the shared representation of the former national currency: the franc is still perceived as the national *money* which symbolises *France*.

### Attitudes toward the euro

In the first phase it was possible to study attitudes through two different steps. First, among the terms spontaneously produced through free association, a large proportion were neutral, some were clearly positive and others were negative. 12.63 per cent of all the evoked terms in the representation of the euro appear to have a negative connotation.

The second step relates to the various Likert scales. By summing the results obtained through the nine scales, the overall attitude toward the euro appears to be neutral for the 52 teenagers, with an average score of 2.42 (1 being totally negative, 5 being totally positive). Individual answers were widely spread, with extreme answers in both directions, thus producing a high dispersion of answers (SD = 1.07).

During the second period, attitudes were only measured by the average score of the nine scales together; the overall attitude toward the euro of the 205 teenagers interviewed is very similar to that observed in the first phase (M = 2.7), which, though slightly more positive, is still close to being neutral with a smaller dispersion of answers (SD = 0.74).

## National or supranational feeling of territorial belonging?

Responses to the question about the feeling of being European show clearly that the responses changed in less than a year. In 1999, results from the European Values Survey showed that only 4 per cent of the subjects selected Europe as their personal choice in terms of belonging.

In the first phase of the study (2001) the tendency of the great majority – 85 per cent – was to agree that, even though 'France belongs to Europe', they felt 'French and not European'. The same open-ended question in phase two, after the introduction of the euro, produced a large majority – 77.28 per cent – who explained that they are European, because they use the same currency as so many other European countries.

The samples – who were not the same teenagers but each sample of which was constituted on the same basis – completely changed to a new type territorial belonging between phase one and two. 85 per cent felt that they belonged to France in phase one, 77 per cent stated that they belonged to Europe seven months later: the difference is striking. This fundamental change is surprising, as though the introduction of a single currency could really, in such a short time, change the feeling of belonging.

A list of 20 countries, among them the 12 countries of the Euro-zone, was included in the second questionnaire. Subjects were asked to circle those countries that were members of the euro-zone. On average, each subject circled ten, with no difference between the boys and the girls. The results show that the level of mis-information is directly related to the distance each country is from France: the closer the country, the more accurate the response. France is identified by all the teenagers as belonging to the euro-zone (205: 100 per cent); then countries that share a common border with France range down to 94.6: Spain (204), Italy (198), Germany (196), and Belgium (194).

These French teenagers are not well informed about the twelve countries in the euro-zone; and are not even certain of which countries are in Europe.

In considering the changes which occurred between the two phases, some comments can be made about gender differences, and some comparisons can be made with two samples of adults who were interviewed in a parallel study, with the same questions asked at the same times (cf. Roland-Lévy, 2002b).

**Table 1: Which countries are using the euro?**
**(205 responses: countries not in the Euro-zone indicated with an asterisk *)**

| Country | number indicating in the Euro-zone | percentage |
|---|---|---|
| France | 205 | 100.0 |
| Spain | 204 | 99.5 |
| Italy | 198 | 96.5 |
| Germany | 196 | 95.6 |
| Belgium | 194 | 94.6 |
| Netherlands | 187 | 91.2 |
| Luxembourg | 185 | 90.2 |
| Portugal | 185 | 90.2 |
| Greece | 157 | 76.6 |
| Austria | 146 | 71.2 |
| Denmark* | 132 | 64.4 |
| Finland | 123 | 60 |
| Ireland | 99 | 48.3 |
| Norway* | 65 | 32.5 |
| Sweden* | 51 | 24.9 |
| UK* | 22 | 10.7 |
| Turkey* | 19 | 9.3 |
| Romania* | 14 | 6.8 |
| Turkey* | 5 | 2.4 |
| Israel* | 2 | – |

## Boys versus girls

There were no significant differences between girls and boys in terms of knowledge about Europe and the euro-zone. The main differences were shown in the general attitude toward the new currency. On a scale of 1 to 5, girls have a neutral attitude regarding the euro (mean = 2.28; SD = 80), whereas boys have a positive attitude (mean = 3.13; SD = 68). Girls and boys in the second phase

157

associated similar terms in their representations of the euro; but when asked to select terms specifically *not* associated with the euro, girls identified the term *conversion*, while the boys did not – the girls appeared to have no problem in adjusting to the new currency. One task asked subjects to give the price in euro of a stamp for an ordinary letter to Europe: the girls knew the precise price (0.46 €), while the boys were less certain. During the first phase, a task required conversions from the franc to the euro, and – unlike the adult sample – both girls and boys were extremely good at this, with a natural spontaneous approximation of prices, as if they already knew how to 'automatically' convert French francs into euros.

The concrete use of the new currency seems to have definitely influenced both boys' and girls' perception of being European rather than just French.

## Comparing teenagers with two samples of adults

In phase one, a sample of 109 adults was also interviewed, half of whom were bankers (57) and half small shopkeepers (52). Bankers had unsurprisingly positive attitudes toward the euro (mean = 3.3; SD = 0.99), while shopkeepers' attitudes toward the yet-to-be introduced currency which was closer to neutral (mean = 2.8; SD = 1.1). In their spontaneous production of terms linked to the euro, shopkeepers produced more negative associations than the samples of bankers and teenagers. Teenagers emphasized not only the positive aspects of *novelty* and *easiness* linked to the euro, but also the *complexity* engendered by the new currency for the older generation.

During phase one, *money* was identified as the central concept for the franc and for the euro, both by adults and teenagers. In phase two, the adult groups shared a common new representation of the euro centred around *Europe, union, new* and *unique*. When looking at the common terms selected as *not* belonging to the representation of the euro, the adults selected *easiness* first, followed by *France* and by *countries*, and then *Dollar*. Teenagers tend to share this representation of the euro focused around *Europe, union* and *new,* except that *unique* is replaced by *money*. When looking at the common terms rejected from the representation of teenagers, three shared terms appear: *Dollar* (also rejected by the adults), and *complexity* and *easiness*.

| Table 2: Representations of the euro by adults and teenagers, 2002 | teenagers | adults |
|---|---|---|
| Representations positively made of the euro | Europe | Europe |
| | union | union |
| | new | new |
| | unique | money |
| Representations not made with the euro | dollar | easiness |
| | complexity | france |
| | easiness | countries |
| | | dollar |

At the beginning of this chapter questions were asked about how much children and young people understood about their economical and political environment. Would this understanding develop in the same way when there was radical social, economic and political change? The data obtained in this study suggests that, through the example of the introduction of a single currency – an important economic and political change – there can be specific and fundamental modifications in terms of political socialisation, producing a much broader feeling of belonging.

As soon as this economic and political change occurred, a new social representation of the euro appeared among teenagers; their general attitude toward the single currency moved towards the positive side of the Likert scales (mean = 2.7), and this is especially true for teenage boys (mean = 3.13). More importantly, these modifications have already affected the feeling of territorial belonging. The use of the single currency clearly turned their previous national feeling of belonging into a new European feeling of belonging.

This radical change in feeling towards a supranational belonging will needs to be checked in the future, as the novelty of the currency may have triggered a phenomenon that is only temporary. This will be tested in a year's time, not only in France, but also in the other countries of the European Monetary Union.

The results of this study may prove to be extremely useful for educators concerned about developing the sense of being a European citizen. They show that tolerance, a respect for others and for cultural differences can be taught and assessed through social representations.

# 10

# European values and political eduction

Jan Kerkhofs

In no other wars have more people of more countries and continents been involved than in the 20th century first and second World Wars. And most of the tens of millions of people killed on the battlefields were young men, having had no say at all in the decisions of the warlords (Davies, 1997).

Though the French Revolution stressed important values such as freedom, equality and brotherhood ('sisterhood' not yet being in the vocabulary), the latter had mainly a nationalist, even a tribal connotation. It is only since the collapse of the fascist states in 1945 that civic education has very slowly entered a minority of schools. If wars are prepared in the minds of people, this is also true of peace. One of the main reasons why I started the Foundation *European Values Study* (EVS) at the end of the seventies was a concern for peace; the EVS covered also North America, but in this contribution we focus upon Europe.[1] Once citizens are taught to stress values other than 'holy' fighting, they will realise how much peace is needed to protect the three principles of the French Revolution mentioned above, on a European as well as on a worldwide scale. Indeed, democracy is built on a balance between these three values. However, this balance is only exceptionally reached. The USA stresses mostly freedom, Russia mostly equality. Since our first survey in 1981 the Europeans have steadily stressed freedom more and equality less. The poorer countries have a tendency to emphasise the latter more, the wealthier ones freedom, since, with economic progress, the preference for freedom increases. Few countries have been able to integrate solidarity satisfactorily.

## Facts and Figures from the Surveys

In this brief overview I will focus on the results of the three EVS surveys (1981, 1990 and 1999–2000) the latter of which covered more than half a billion Europeans, including Russians and Ukrainians. The statistics given refer mainly to the 1999–2000 survey. The youngest age group polled was of those between 18 and 30. In the context of this chapter it is striking that 'tolerance' has become steadily more important, a value much needed for our multicultural and multi-religious society. We presented all the interviewees with a list of eleven qualites out of which they had to choose the five they considered most important for the education of their children at home. Three times, in all the age groups and in almost all the countries, the following have been mentioned as being of primary importance: tolerance, a sense of responsibility and good manners. All three are social values and absolutely necessary for life in society. In the 1981 survey we added 'honesty'. This quality was at that time mentioned as by far the most important one. But this first survey covered only Western Europe.

Here we have to add a warning. Tolerance has a double meaning, positive as well as negative. We can and should tolerate the existence of different religions, but not the oppression of women by religion; we can and should tolerate a plurality of political parties, but, as Umberto Eco once said, we have to be intolerant regarding the people who deny the Holocaust and the concentration camps. People who tolerate this undermine democracy with a culture of dishonesty and lies. Fortunately, our surveys revealed that, in all the countries and across the generations, people prefer, among all the political systems, democracy, even if they complain about its lack of efficiency.

Tolerance means pluralism. And pluralism is a consequence of individualisation, a process that characterises more and more the

European state of mind. However, individualisation doesn't automatically mean individualism. More than 90 per cent, particularly among the younger generation, say they want to support movements defending human rights as well as peace and care for the environment. The overwhelming majority declare that they will help handicapped people and the elderly. Though in some countries a substantial minority does not want immigrants or people of another race or religion 'as neighbours' (e.g. in Poland), this minority is shrinking and is particularly small among younger people and among the better educated. We are far from the previous mentality of '*Gott mit uns*', '*Dieu avec nous*,' or '*Dios con nosotros*', when God was on the side of the nationalists.

However, one must not to be naive. Democracy means politics, and thus participation in public life and commitment to accepting a whole range of duties. On a list of six domains presented to our sample of Europeans, family comes first, work second, followed by friends, leisure and religion, while politics comes last. Only in two countries does a majority consider politics as very or quite important (57 per cent in the Netherlands and 55 per cent in Sweden). The least interested are southern and eastern European countries.[2] Asked if they are interested in politics, 54 per cent of the Europeans say *no* (in France 63 per cent, in Great Britain 62 per cent, in Russia 61 per cent, in Germany and Denmark 39 per cent, in the Czech Republic 30 per cent). The difference between the generations is not significant. When raising the problem of confidence in the major institutions, few Europeans trust their parliaments: for Europe as a whole, only 35 per cent (in the Netherlands 55 per cent, in Sweden 51 per cent, but in France only 40 per cent, in Germany and Great Britain 35 per cent, in Russia and Romania 19 per cent). Though trust in the European Union has decreased after the well-known 'scandals', people have more confidence in the Union than in their own national parliaments, namely 43 per cent (Italy and Portugal close to 70 per cent, Belgium, Luxembourg, Spain, Ireland, Greece, Malta, Slovakia and Hungary more than 50 per cent). Ukraine reaches 45 per cent, Russia only 25 per cent. With 51 per cent, people clearly trust the United Nations more than the European Union.

Notwithstanding this outspoken lack of trust in parliament, which is still the main democratic institution, the vast majority refuse to deliver the country to a strong leader who would not have to bother about a parliament or elections, and still less to an army. As Winston Churchill once said, democracy remains the lesser evil.

In spite of this lack of interest in politics, in many parts of Europe the so-called 'civil society' is not passive or fatalistic. In Western Europe, with the exception of southern countries such as Greece, Spain and Portugal, a majority believe that individuals should take more responsibility in providing for themselves, while in Central Europe, with the exception of the Czech Republic and Romania, a majority feel that the state should take more responsibility to ensure that everyone is provided for. Fewer people in Central Europe than in western Europe say that they want more say in important government decisions or say that freedom of speech should be protected. In recent decades we have witnessed in the western part an explosion of all kinds of networks, initiated by the citizens themselves, with people of all ages starting movements and organisations from the bottom up. Groups of volunteers are steadily increasing their membership. This is more particularly the case for Northern Europe, especially in the Netherlands and in Flanders. To give one example: in the Netherlands Greenpeace has close to 700,000 supporters, *Médecins sans Frontières* about 600,000. Many thousands back Amnesty International. Women are becoming more vocal everywhere and refuse the old patriarchal style. However, one has to admit that in most countries the younger generation is less involved than the older generations and youth organisations attract fewer members than half a century ago. Here the consequences of individualisation become visible. Young people prefer an involvement that is limited in time.

The surveys also show that the tendency to protest is on the increase. The percentage of those who sign petitions, want to join boycotts or to organise lawful or wild-cat strikes has been growing during the last two decades, which undoubtedly means a willingness to participate. People in firms and offices want more and more to be convinced about the validity of the instructions given, and not simply to obey orders.

Under the influence of the tendency to individualisation some people complain, too easily, that there is no longer any civic sense. The findings of the surveys show, on the contrary, that the majority of the Europeans still accept a great number of obligations, important for survival of a society in which solidarity is not an idle word. From a list of many kinds of behaviours, the interviewees were asked to select those they considered as acceptable and those which were not. We find that only a minority gave negative answers on items dealing with the common good. And though the younger ones declare they are more 'permissive' than the older ones, most by far say they consider throwing litter or smoking in public places is not acceptable; they reject tax evasion, driving under the influence of alcohol, exceeding speed limits in towns and cities, using drugs, or evading fares for public transport. Of course, we know that there is often a gap between opinions and behaviours. Nevertheless, the picture is a clear one: young people want ethical behaviour in the public sphere. Though reliable figures are difficult to collect, every year billions of euros are willingly given to those who suffer either in one's own country or in developing countries, though few know that more than four billion people still have to live on less than 2.5 euros a day.

## Teaching civic responsibility

According to the EVS, no institution in Europe is granted more confidence than the education system, with 71 per cent having 'a great deal' and 'quite a lot' of confidence, particularly among the younger generation. Here again, differences according to regions are striking. We find the highest figures (between 75 per cent and 85 per cent) in the Nordic countries, Ireland, Austria, Poland, Belgium and the Netherlands. The lowest levels of confidence in the education system are found in the Czech Republic and in Italy, with 54 per cent, and particularly in Greece (37 per cent).

The data about the lack of political participation suggest that too little is done on teaching civics and promoting civic responsibility, though teachers and children are also citizens. As everyone knows, most schools are traditionally rather conservative institutions in society. Often they appear extremely repetitive. Tradition prevails, even if more and more computers enter the classrooms, even if children have their own mobile phones and communicate at home with e-mails. The real danger is that children become isolated cells in the body of society. Half a century ago most children had two or three sisters or brothers, enabling them to become socialised at home, but today there is no European country where women under the age of 45 reach the replacement figure of an average of 2.1 children – though the EVS reports that most people in all age groups consider 2.5 as the ideal number. In Germany, Spain and Italy the number of children is most often a single child. This child can be spoiled as a little god. Moreover the increasing divorce rate loosens family links. This whole process tends not only towards individualisation, but also towards individualism. The 'I' thus becomes more important than the 'we'. A democratic society is based on a respect for the 'we', for the otherness of the other. It implies everywhere give and take, a mixture of rights and duties. In many parts of Europe there has been a dwindling of the traditional youth organisations which were the laboratories of socialisation.

Though we have to accept that schools cannot replace the family and youth organisations as places for a healthy socialisation train-ing, for many young people they have become the main centres where serious socialisation is offered. It is not an easy task. Indeed, too many teachers suffer from burn-out syndrome: youngsters are more nervous than in the past (they don't sleep enough!), they seem less obedient (in our scales 'obedience' scores very low in their age group), less willing to become participants in education projects. Schools complain about pupils despising one another, giving in to all kinds of hedonism, looking for drugs, alcohol and early sex (the phenomenon of teenage pregnancies), etc. All this means that, probably more than in the past, strict teaching will have to be counterbalanced by education in which values are embedded, including civic understanding. Education means introducing team-work, helping youngsters to accept limitations and to assume responsibilities. This education has to be tackled at four levels.

First of all, every school needs an education project, a kind of 'mission statement'. The staff has to accept that it is not enough to train pupils for the economic and technical world of tomorrow, to enable them to enter schools of higher learning, to live with the per-spective of a good salary and to enjoy everything the consumer society offers. Teachers have to show that life in society means commitment to that society, and primarily within the small society of the school. Teachers themselves will have to offer strong models of civic understanding, not only by what they teach, but even more by their own examples: how they support their colleagues, how they accept supplementary tasks, how they behave in a polite way, how they oppose sexism, how they listen to complaints, how they take care of the environment in the classroom, or how they deal with pupils facing problems, personal and at home.

Two elements seem here of the utmost importance: identity and tolerance.

Identity means that teachers accept the fact that they belong to a region, rural or urban, with few or many jobless people, with few or many immigrants, with or without social tensions, and the fact that they belong to a democratic state. They have to know that this state is not perfect, that patriotism is a virtue but closed nationalism a vice and that political extremism is a danger. And they need a wider horizon. Young people will quickly learn to live with the euro, because they travel much more than their parents or grandparents (see Chapter 9 by Roland-Lévy). But they need as well a sense of European citizenship. Teachers who have not integrated this citizenship, in their lessons but also through contacts abroad, by learning other languages, by meeting colleagues across the borders, are not well prepared for introducing pupils to an unavoidable future. It is here that I would introduce a strong plea for not giving in to a trend that tries to reduce the lessons of history. Who can understand the differences between northern, southern and eastern Europe without an insight into Europe's past? Who will be able to interpret what is going on in the Balkans if they do not know why so many old devils are still at work in the minds of the people who live there? The past is still alive in the debates within the European Commission and the European Parliament, but also in the many prejudices opposing the Europeans with a Christian tradition to the Muslims in our midst. It is striking that among the three major regional communities in Belgium, Brussels is the most 'religious' one, thanks to the presence of Muslims.

Tolerance is the second most important factor. According to the latest *Eurobarometer* the least tolerant countries regarding minorities in the European Union, are in decreasing order: Greece, Belgium, Denmark, France and Germany. Nevertheless, when compared with previous surveys, it is obvious that the Europeans are becoming steadily *more* tolerant. Our education towards a civic understanding has to consider the near future. Willy-nilly our pupils will face a multicultural and multi-religious society. Christians will have to live with people having another view of the world, native Europeans will have to live with migrants. Let us illustrate this with a few figures. Today in France 70 per cent of the night service in hospitals is taken care of by non-French doctors (and 30 per cent of the whole medical staff is non-French). About 20 per cent of the British have 'black genes'. Without more migrants the economy and the social security system could collapse in many European countries. If Turkey, which is already a member of NATO and of the Council of Europe, becomes, around 2025, a member of the European Union, which is even accepted by its old enemy Greece and promoted by president Prodi, it will be, with 87 million people at that time, the most important member of the Union. Soon Muslim nurses will take care of elderly European people. There will be more and more mixed marriages. Are our teaching staffs prepared for these enormous transformations? Young gifted students as well as professors will have to work with so-called 'coloured people', as workers are already doing in the factories. A similar process is developing quickly in the US, and, more slowly in Russia, where Moscow has already 10 per cent Muslims. Sport teams and restaurants are already multicultural. Soon our schools and universities will be. In some of our city schools 90 per cent of the pupils are children of immigrants. The teaching staff will become more and more diverse. The whole process will have enormous consequences for our democracies and for our training toward an updated civic sense.

One may add that an education project implies some kind of global view. Very often this is lacking. Unlike the past, most schools in Europe today – Belgium excepted – are state schools or depend on local authorities. They often opt for ideological 'neutrality', and most teachers and parents share a relativistic ideology. According to the EVS, only 31 per cent of the Europeans declare 'that there are absolutely clear guidelines about what is good and evil, and these always apply to everyone, whatever the circumstances.' A clear majority of 62 per cent declare 'that there can never be absolutely clear guidelines about what is good and evil; and what is good and evil depends entirely upon the circumstances at the time.' Only in Poland and in Malta is this majority small, while it is overwhelming in the Nordic countries. When looking at the age groups, we find that the youngest follow the Nordic viewpoint, much more so than their parents or grandparents. This understandable uncertainty about principles will affect any education project, and certainly in matters of civic understanding.

Secondly, parents have to be backed in order to face all these challenges. As the EVS reveals, most parents are primarily rooted in the small territory of the village or the town. A small minority mention the wider world and even fewer Europe: they have to widen their horizons. This means an ongoing dialogue with them. Too few schools have accepted the input of parents' councils. Parents too have to assent to the education project of the school and have to assume their co-responsibility. Many fear the trend towards a multicultural society and know little or nothing about the real advantages of European integration. Often they are only looking for a good diploma. They are afraid that the presence of boys and girls of other cultural backgrounds will lower the standards, even promote mixed marriages. Parents try to defend their children, even against the teachers and the school, and thus undermine discipline. A school that is not seriously supported by parents is often powerless. On the other hand, when a school succeeds in building a creative relationship with parents, the climate fosters constructive attitudes, between teachers and pupils and between pupil and pupil. Parents who have a responsibility in politics or in economic and social life should talk about their experiences, join panel discussions and build bridges between school life and public life.

Thirdly, the pupils have to accept that they belong to a team, not only in sports or when they co-operate in drama, but also in specific learning activities. They belong to a team in time and in space. First, in time. Nations and states, as well as Europe itself, are historical constructs. They are rooted in the dreams, as well as in the tragedies and the horrors of a long past. They are supported and handicapped by old memories, hidden treasures and heavy burdens. The EVS shows that most people are proud to belong to their country, but also reveals that in some countries the disaster of the Second World War hinders a healthy pride, while in others chauvinism awakens old prejudices. For both groups a healing process is needed.

Pupils also belong to a team in space. Young people have to be taught that all the territorial levels they belong to (town, region, nation, Europe, the whole world) are interrelated, not only by the food they eat, through the pictures they see and the folk songs they hear, but mainly by the sheer fact of being human. What happens in Eastern Europe affects the western part; the dramatic situation of Central Africa is reflected in the faces of the black brothers and sisters we meet on the streets of our cities, and daily, everyone is forced to become aware of the fact that one in three citizens of our globe is either Chinese or Indian. The children of today will soon be real world citizens.[3]

This reality should enter the classrooms – not in order to over-burden pupils with an unbearable responsibility, but to enrich them with a feeling of universal sisterhood and brotherhood. This forces teachers and pupils to combine a double feeling, the one of belonging to a national cultural identity and the one of being citizens of the blue planet. This feeling will have to be reflected in a plurality of languages. In January 2000 the British weekly *The Economist* stated in an article that three languages would remain for communication, namely English, Mandarin Chinese and Spanish. As was Latin in Europe for many centuries, English has already become the 'koinè' at world level. To find a balance between our national idioms and English is a challenge and a great opportunity. Indeed, the first bridge for meeting other people in space is a common language. At the same time, Europe means a mix of unity and of diversity. All the surveys show that the Europeans do not want a European control of their national cultures, of which the protection of our many languages is the basic pillar. The defence of this diversity is as important as the promotion of a common linguistic tool.

Furthermore, a long tradition has stressed competition in our schools: obtaining good results was often the main goal. Thus individualism has been fostered. Everyone had to fight for him or herself. We see in the EVS that, when most people are afraid of too much competition and want more solidarity, at the same time a majority still favour the blessings of competition, of increasing one's income. Nevertheless, real life teaches that nothing important can be achieved without teamwork, surely not in a world which has steadily become more complex. Too often, no good models are offered to learn to work in teams and to collaborate for a common and shared success. Moreover, this gives an occasion for developing good leadership and for accepting it.

Allow me to introduce here a tricky problem, that of the defence forces. According to the EVS, two countries, the US and Russia,

171

trust most, among all their institutions, the army and the church. The army is surely a national symbol. A majority in most European countries – also mainly among the younger age groups – say that they trust the army a great deal or quite a lot (particularly, with more than 80 per cent, in Finland, Great Britain and Romania). But in several countries only a minority agrees (less than 40 per cent in the Czech Republic, in Estonia, Austria, Belgium and the Netherlands – in the latter two countries the peace movement is the strongest). For centuries the army was an idol. The acceptance of the Declaration of Human Rights in San Francisco (1948) was a turning point. However, peace is still threatened in many parts of the globe. And peace has to be defended. Today in many countries compulsory military service has been abolished; it is often difficult to find enough volunteers for the army or for the Euro-corps. Nevertheless, we need a defence system, even an army for peace-keeping and for necessary intervention in troubled regions. Whereas 56 per cent of the Europeans trust their national armed forces, only 41 per cent say they trust NATO. This trust is particularly low in Greece, in Austria, in Spain and, naturally, in Russia and Belarus. But young people express more trust in NATO than do the older generations. They should be encouraged to become still more aware of the positive side of the 'blue helmets' at the service of the United Nations or NATO – in Europe 51 per cent do trust the UN, and close to 60 per cent among young people. School could help in opening pupils' eyes for a new kind of defence for peace, thus serving democracy and the enormous value of freedom. A survey in France (2001) shows the three items that rank highest among those guaranteeing peace are firstly, economic and social development; secondly, international justice and solidarity; and thirdly, education, both secular and religious. These are considered as the basis for a culture of peace. Asked about the means to stop and limit the trend towards violence, two thirds mentioned: 'by favouring the building of a united Europe'.

Finally, a school is not an island. It is located in a neighbourhood, which reveals the bright and the dark sides of society: parks, playgrounds, sporting facilities, as well as criminality, lack of care for the environment, dangerous traffic, often fear of the unknown. Racism and sexism undermine life in society, and one's neighbourhood is an image of the whole world. Therefore, education also means opening the eyes to see what is happening nearby or far away and offering the beginning of small-scale, though efficient, answers. It struck me that the Catholic aid agency Cafod in the UK devotes six percent of its budget to its awareness and education programme in England and Wales. The programme includes education for justice in schools. The children saw that if something was not done to change the way they live, the dreams of their peers in the Third World for a share in the good things of creation could never be realised. The vision of a just and sustainable world is not out of reach. It can be achieved – and this idea is a challenge for young people. Pupils should be assisted in debating these problems, helped to analyse the reasons behind them and to become creative in developing a response at an appropriate level.

So far, children have had no right to participate in national or local elections, though these can be important for their future. Is it unthinkable for them to plan a meeting with people of the town council, to be informed about what is planned and to be allowed to their remarks? It can be done in a way that is both playful and serious. Parents' councils could back it. Schools could open opportunities for service to the community, not only during holidays but also as a part of the teaching itself. Other possible commitments might include choirs visiting houses for the elderly to perform to them, children organising theatre plays for disabled children of their own age, setting up exhibitions of their best pictures, films and paintings, and starting their own school periodicals and becoming publishers. The more able pupils can spend time helping the less gifted and should be encouraged to do so.

By all these and many other means, young people have to integrate a hierarchy of values (Domenach, 1989). In a 'zapping' culture everything is likely to become relative and many people are lost in a labyrinth of ideologies offered by the market place. Of course, one cannot teach 'values' as a specific subject. Values will have to be transmitted in all the lessons and above all by the personal style of the teacher and by the whole atmosphere of the school. It remains extremely important that pupils, on leaving their school, have a solid backbone, enabling them to survive as social and responsible persons amidst the many tensions and contradictions of life.

In an article in *The Tablet* (Talbot, 1999) Marianne Talbot, a member of the British government's Advisory Group on Citizenship raised the question: 'Can values be taught?' Some doubt it and proclaim that there are no common values anymore and that, as a consequence, secular schools cannot teach them.

> This [writes Talbot] is a pseudo problem. In 1997, the National Forum for Values in Education and the Community, made up of 150 people of diverse ethnic, religious and cultural backgrounds, drafted a statement of agreed values. The polling organisation *Mori* sent this draft to 3,200 schools and 700 national organisations. They had also conducted focus groups of parents, head-teachers and governors, and an omnibus poll of 1,500 adults. Of the respondents, 97 percent said they agreed with the statement of values and would like to see them taught in schools.

To teach the values of good citizenship, schools need not fit new material into the school day and overburden both teachers and pupils. Talbot describes what can be done:

> Social and moral responsibility are caught as well as taught ... In explaining unpopular decisions, adjudicating quarrels, listening to the sad and disaffected and reprimanding the recalcitrant, teachers are modelling the behaviour of responsible adults and making clear the difference between right and wrong. In observing the consequences of disobeying rules, in their playground spats and classroom negotiations, pupils are learning what behaviour is, and what is not, socially acceptable.

Is Talbot over-optimistic? I don't think so. She rightly added that the examples of teachers, of parents and of the larger community remain of utmost importance. I would add the example of youth movements. I will only give one example I know well. Each Boy

Scout or Girl Guide is a member, first of all, of the small patrol, where everyone has a concrete responsibility and is strictly controlled in a fair way. The leader of the group is only a kind of liaison officer. This is where the famous principle of subsidiarity, so important in community life at every level, finds its concrete application.

## Conclusion

Robert Bellah, the American social scientist, has developed the main theme of this chapter in his book *The Good Society* (Bellah, 1992). This is an impressive plea for more commitment to the 'Common Good'. Bellah stresses the fact that society relies on institutions: he mentions the market and organised work, the government, the law and the Churches. But above all he emphasises education, technical as well as moral. 'We must recover an enlarged paradigm of knowledge, which recognises the value of science but acknowledges that other ways of knowing have equal dignity. Practical reason, in its classical sense of moral reason, must regain its importance in our educational life.'

I would like to add the European Union to his list of institutions. As I have mentioned, it did strike me that in our surveys Europeans have more confidence in the European Union than in their own national parliaments. Which means that for them, Europe is a symbol of hope, of their main values of freedom, equality and solidarity. It is on this hope that a solid education project can be built.

One of my great teachers is Vaclav Havel, the president of the Czech Republic and one of the founding fathers of the famous liberation movement *Charta '77*. In an address to the nation he said:

> Let us teach ourselves and others that politics ought to be a reflection of the aspiration to contribute to the happiness of the community and not of the need to deceive and pillage the community. Let us teach both ourselves and others that politics does not have to be the art of the possible, especially if this means the art of speculating, calculating, secret agreements, and pragmatic

manoeuvring, but that it also can be the art of the impossible, that is the art of making both ourselves and the world better. (Havel, 1990)

Convinced, after the disaster of the Second World War, that one had to try the impossible, Jean Monnet, Robert Schuman, Konrad Adenauer, Alcide de Gasperi and later many other great leaders such as Jacques Delors, have been inspired by this realistic utopia. It is this vision which should be in the mind of every teacher.

## Notes

1. For more information: EVS, Tilburg University, P. O. Box 90153, NL-Tilburg (Website: evs.kub.nl) and L. Halman, *The European Values Study: A Third Wave* (Source Book of the 1999/2000 European Values Study Surveys, Tilburg University, 2001).

2. For the youngest age group politics seem even less important than for their parents: e.g. Russia 18–30: 29 per cent, 46–60 years: 44 per cent; Ukraine: 31 per cent and 41 per cent; Flanders: 24 per cent and 36 per cent; Ireland: 25 per cent and 37 per cent.

3. A serious civic sense implies trust. The EVS shows that trust in other people is, in general, very weak. For Europe people declare they trust 'very much and much': 83 per cent their own family, 29 per cent people in their neighbourhood, 21 per cent in their region, 24 per cent their countrymen, 26 per cent mankind and only 12 per cent the Europeans. Young people admit a little more trust than the older generations.

# Notes on Contributors

**Ian Davies** is Senior Lecturer in Educational Studies at the University of York. He is the co-author or editor of a number of articles and books on citizenship including *Good Citizenship and Educational Provision*, *Teaching the Holocaust* and *Teaching Citizenship through Secondary History*.

**David Edye** is Senior Lecturer in Politics at London Metropolitan University and a visiting lecturer at the Université Paul-Valéry, Montpellier. He is co-author (with Valerio Lintner) of *Contemporary Europe (1996)* and has written widely on issues concerning young people and European citizenship.

**Hélène Feertchak** is a Senior Lecturer in Social Psychology at the University Rene Descartes Paris 5. She is member of GERPA (a research laboratory studying child psychology, from the Institute of Psychology) where she mainly conducts surveys on young people's values. She is the author of *Les motivations et les valeurs en psycho-sociologie*.

**Carole Hahn** is professor of educational studies at Emory University in Atlanta, USA. She teaches graduate and undergraduate courses in social studies education and comparative education and conducts research on comparative civic education. Professor Hahn was the National Research Coordinator for the United States portion of the IEA Civic Education Study and she is author of the book *Becoming political: Comparative Perspectives on Citizenship Education*. She is a past president of the National Council for the Social Studies.

**Aristotle Kallis** is a political scientist who is currently completing his PhD on 'Irredentism in nineteenth and twentieth century Europe' in the Department of Politics at the University of Edinburgh.

**Jan Kerkhofs** was born in Hasselt, Belgium in 1924, and is a former Professor of General Sociology (Antwerp University), and now Emeritus Professor of Theology at the Catholic University Leuven. He was the founder of the 'European Values Study Foundation' based in Tilburg

University, Netherlands. He is the author of some 50 books and hundreds of articles.

**Maureen Killeavy** is a Lecturer in the Education Department, University College Dublin. She has extensive experience as a teacher at all levels in the education system. She is a member of the Expert Advisory Group on Post Primary Teacher Education in Ireland and the National Policy Advisory and Development Committee she and she has served on the Ministerial Commission on the Points System. She is Vice-President of the Association of Teacher Education in Europe and Vice-President of the Irish Federation of University Teachers.

**Christine Roland-Lévy** has been Senior Lecturer in Social Psychology since 1990, at the University Rene Descartes Paris 5, where she is member of GRASP (a research laboratory studying the relations between social psychology and the economic world, in the Institute of Psychology). She was president of the *International Association for Research in Economic Psychology* (IAREP, 1997–1999) and is currently president of the *Economic Psychology Division of the International Association of Applied Psychology* (IAAP, 2002–2006). She has written a series of articles, chapters and books, including *Psychologie Économique. Théories et Applications* and *Everyday Representations of the Economy.*

**Alistair Ross** is Professor of Education at the London Metropolitan University (formerly the University of North London), where he is Director of the Institute for Policy Studies in Education and the international co-ordinator of the CiCe (Children's Identity and Citizenship in Europe) Thematic Network. He has research interests in the school curriculum (author of *Curriculum: Construction and Critique*) children's political and social learning, on the careers of teachers, citizenship education, and on access to higher education. He is series editor for *European Issues in Children's Identity and Citizenship.*

**Tony Thorpe** has worked for the Citizenship Foundation since it was established in 1989. He has written and co-authored a range of citizenship teaching materials, including *Understanding Citizenship* and the *Young Citizen's Passport.*

# Bibliography

Abric, J. C. (1976) *Jeux, conflits et représentations sociales*, Thèse d'Etat, Aix-en-Provence: Université de Provence.

Abric, J. C. (1994) Les représentations sociales: aspects théoriques, in J. C. Abric (ed) *Pratiques sociales et représentations*, Paris: Presses Universitaires de France, pp. 10–36.

Adams, R. (1972) *Watership Down*. London: Collins (Penguin/Puffin, 1973).

Ahier, J. and Ross, A. (1994) (eds.) *The Social Subjects in the Curriculum*, London: Falmer.

Ahonen, S. (2001) Forming a Collective Identity through Historical Memories. Research Project 'The No-History Generation?' pp 91–108, in J. van der Leeuw-Roord (ed) *History for Today and Tomorrow: What does Europe mean for School History?* Hamburg: Korber-Stiftung.

Almond, G. and Verba, S. (1965) *The Civic Culture: political attitudes and democracy in five nations,* Boston: Little, Brown and Co.

Anderson, B. (1983) *Imagined Communities: Reflections on the origins and spread of nationalism,* London: Verso.

Antonouris, G. (1990) *The European Dimension in Teacher Training, Activity Book 2: An Introductory Course on InterculturalCross-curricular Themes: National Curriculum, Environmental Issues.* Nottingham: Nottingham Polytechnic.

Aron, R. (1974) Is Multinational Citizenship possible? *Social Research,* vol. 4, 41, no. 4, pp. 638–656.

Badie, B. and Perrineau, P. (2000) Citoyens au-delà de l'État, introduction, in B. Badie and P. Perrineau, (eds.) *Le citoyen. Mélanges offerts à Alain Lancelot*, Paris: Presses de Sciences Po.

Baldi, S., Perie, M., Skidmore, D., Greenberg, E. and Hahn, C. (2001) *What democracy means to ninth-graders: U.S. results from the international IEA civic education study,* Washington, D.C.: National Center for Education Statistics, U.S. Department of Education. http://nces.ed.gov/surveys/cived. Order from U.S. Department of Education, ED Pubs, P.O. Box 1398, Jessup MD 20794–1398.

Batho, G. (1990) The History of Teaching of Civics and Citizenship in England, *The Curriculum Journal,* 1, pp. 91–100.

Beernaert, Y., van Dijk, H. and Sander, Th. (1993) *The European Dimension in Teacher Education,* Brussels: Association for Teacher Education in Europe (ATEE)/RIF).

Bell, D. (1973) *The coming of Post-industrial society: a venture in social forecasting,* New York: Basic Books.

Bell, D. (1976) *The cultural contradictions of capitalism*, New York: Basic Books.

Bell, G. H. (1995) (ed) *Educating European Citizens: citizenship values and the European dimension,* London: David Fulton.

Bellah, R. (ed) (1992) *The Good Society,* New York: Vintage.

Blair, T. (1996) *New Britain: My Vision of a Young Country*, London: Fourth Estate.

Bloch, M. (1928) 'Pour une histoire comparée des sociétés européennes', *Revue de Synthèse Historique,* 46, pp. 15–50.

Blunket, D. (1999) Letter to Schools, *Consultation on the Secretary of State's proposals for a revised national curriculum in England*, London: DfEE, May 1999.

Borhaug, K. (1999) Education for Democracy, in A. Ross (ed) *Young Citizens in Europe,* London: CiCe.

Bowles, S and Gintis, H. (1976) *Schooling in Capitalist America: Educational Reform and the Contradictions of Economic Life*, New York: Basic Books.

Boy, D. and Mayer, N. (1997) *L'électeur français en questions*, Paris: Presses de Sciences Po.

Bréchon, P. (2000) L'univers des valeurs politiques, chap. 6, in P. Bréchon (ed) *Les valeurs des Français. Évolutions de 1980 à 2000*, Paris: Armand Colin.

Bruner, J. and Haste, H. (eds.) (1987) *Making Sense: The Child's Construction of the World*, London: Methuen.

Castles, S. and Davidson, A (2000) *Citizenship and Migration. Globalisation and the Politics of Belonging,* London: Macmillan.

Cloonan, M. and Davies, I. (1998) Improving the possibility of better teaching by investigating the nature of student learning: with reference to procedural understanding in politics in higher education, *Teaching in Higher Education*, 3, 2, pp. 173–83.

Clough, N., Menter, I. and Tarr, J. (1995) Developing Citizenship Education Programmes, in Latvia in A. Osler, H.F. Rathenow and H. Starkey (eds.) *Teaching for Citizenship in Education*, Stoke on Trent: Trentham.

Colley, L. (1992) *Britons: Forging the Nation, 1707–1837*. Cambridge Ma: Yale University Press.

Colley, L. (1999) Britishness in the 21st Century www.number-10.gov.uk

Commission on Citizenship (1990) *Encouraging Citizenship*, London: HMSO.

Cornbleth, C. (2001) Climates of constraint/restraint of teachers and teaching, in W.B. Stanley (ed), *Critical issues in social studies research for the 21st century,* Greenwich, CT: Information Age Publishing. pp. 73–95.

Council of Europe (1999) *Towards a pluralist and tolerant approach to teaching history: a range of sources and new didactics,* New York: Manhattan Publishing House.

Crick, B. (1974) Basic Political Concepts and Curriculum Development, *Teaching Politics*, 3, 1, pp. 13–24.

Crick, B. and Lister, I. (1978) Political Literacy in B. Crick and A. Porter (eds.) *Political Education and Political Literacy*, London: Longman.

Crick, B. and Porter, A. (1978) *Political education and political literacy,* London: Longman, for the Hansard Society.

Davies, I. (1994) Whatever happened to political education? *Educational Review,* 46, pp. 29–38.

Davies, I. (1999) What has happened in the teaching of politics in schools in England in the last three decades and why? *Oxford Review of Education,* 25, 1 and 2, pp. 125–40.

Davies, I., Gregory, I. and Riley, S.C. (1999) *Good Citizenship and Educational Provision,* London: Falmer.

Davies, N. (1997) *Europe: A History*, London: Pimlico.

Davies, N. (1999) *The Isles*, London: Macmillan.

Degenne, A. (1985) Présentation de l'analyse de similitude, *Informatique et sciences humaines*, 15, pp. 67, 7–26.

Degenne, A. and Vergès, P. (1973) Introduction à l'analyse de similitude, *Revue Française de Sociologie*, 14, pp. 471–512.

Delgado-Moreira, J. M. (1997) European Politics of Citizenship, in the *Qualitative Report,* Vol. 3, No. 3 www.nova.edu/ssss/QR/QR3-3/delgado.html

Delgado-Moreira, J. M. (2000) *Multicultural Citizenship of the European Union,* Aldershot: Ashgate.

Denscombe, M. and Conway, L. (1982) Autonomy and Control in Curriculum Innovation: A Case study of Development Education in the Primary School, *Teaching Politics*, 11, 3, pp. 289–300.

Department of Education and Science (1990) *A View of the Curriculum,* London: HMSO.

Dirn, L. (1990) *La société française en tendances*, Paris: Presses Universitaires de France.

Domenach, J.M. (1989) *Ce qu'il faut enseigner,* Paris: Editions du Seuil, pp. 151–171.

Duchesne, S. (1997) *Citoyenneté à la française*, Paris: Presses de Sciences Po.

Durkheim, E. (1898) Représentations individuelles et représentations collectives (edition of 1967) *Sociologie et Philosophie,* Paris: Presses Universitaires de France.

Easton, D. and Dennis, J. (1969) *Children in the Political System: Origins of Political Legitimacy*, N.Y.: McGraw-Hill.

Ehman, L. (1969) An analysis of the relationships of selected educational variables with the political socialization of high school students, *American Educational Research Journal,* 6, pp. 559–580.

Engle, S. H. and Ochoa, A. (1988) *Education for democratic citizenship: Decision-making in the social studies,* New York: Teachers College Press.

Entwistle, H. (1973) Towards an Educational Theory of Political Socialisation, Paper presented at the *Philosophy of Education Society conference*, New Orleans, USA, 15 April.

European Commission (1994) *Profiles of the RIF Sub-Networks – Network of Training Institution; Profils des sous-réseaux du RIF – Réseau d'institutions de formation.* Luxembourg: Office for Official Publications of the European Communities.

European Commission (2001) *A New Impetus for Youth.* (COM (2001) 681. Brussels: European Commission.

European Commission. (2001) *European Governance – A White Paper* (COM (2001) 428. Brussels: European Commission.

European Research Group on Training for School Exchanges (ERGTSE) (19XX) *Teaching for Exchanges – Aims and Ways of Teacher Training. Encounters for Training.*

Evans, R. W. and Saxe, D. W. (eds.) (1996) *Handbook on teaching issues-centered social studies,* Washington, D.C.: National Council for the Social Studies.

Fischer, F. (1967) *Germany's aims in the First World War.* London: Weidenfeld and Nicolson.

Fischer, F. (1975) *Weltmacht oder Niedergang English / World power or decline the controversy over 'Germany's aims in the First World War'* London: Weidenfeld and Nicolson.

Flament, C. (1962) L'analyse de similitude, *Cahiers du Centre de Recherche Opérationnelle,* 4, pp. 63–97.

Flament, C. (1981) L'analyse de similitude: une technique pour les recherches sur les représentations sociales, *Cahiers de psychologie cognitive,* I (4), pp. 375–395.

*Forever in the shadow of Hitler? original documents of the Historikerstreit, the controversy concerning the singularity of the Holocaust* (1993) Atlantic Highlands, NJ: Humanities Press.

Frey, H. (1999) Rebuilding France: Gaullist historiography, the rise-fall myth and French identity (1945–58). in S. Berger, M. Donovan and K. Passmore (eds), *Writing National Histories: Western Europe since 1800.* pp 205–216. London: Routledge.

Gellner, E. (1983) *Nations and Nationalism,* Oxford: Blackwell.

Giddens, A. (1991) *Modernity and Self-Identity: Self and Society in the Late Modern Age,* London: Polity Press.

Goodson, I. (1997) The educational researcher as public intellectual: modernist dinosaur or postmodernist prospect? The Stenhouse lecture, *British Educational Research Association annual conference,* University of York, September.

Government of Ireland (1988) *Education Act,* Dublin: Stationary Office.

Government of Ireland (2000) *Equal Status Act,* Dublin: Stationary Office.

Government of Ireland (2000) *White Paper on Adult Education: Learning for Life,* Dublin: Stationary Office.

Grimm, D. (1997) *Does Europe Need a Constitution?* in P. Gowan and P. Anderson, *The Question of Europe,* London: Verso.

Grosser, A. (2000) La difficile citoyenneté, chap. 11, in B. Badie and P. Perrineau (eds.) *Le citoyen. Mélanges offerts à Alain Lancelot,* Paris: Presses de Sciences Po.

Guimelli, C. (1989) Pratiques nouvelles et transformation sans rupture d'une représentation sociale: la représentation de la chasse et de la nature, in J. L. Beauvois, R. V. Joule and J. M. Monteil (eds.) *Perspectives cognitives et conduites sociales*. 2. *Représentations et processus sociocritiques*, Cousset: Del Val, pp. 117–141.

Habermas, J. (1981) *Theorie des kommunikativen Handels*, Frankfurt am Main: Suhrkamp.

Habermas, J. (1992) Citizenship and National Identity: Some Reflections on the Future of Europe, *Praxis International,* 12, 1, pp. 1–19.

Habermas, J. (2001) *The Postnational Constellation*, Cambridge: Polity.

Hagtvet, B. and Kuhnl, R. (1980) Contemporary approaches to Fascism: a survey of para-digms, in S.U. Larsen, B. Hagtvet and J.P. Myklebust (eds.) *Who Were the Fascists: Social Roots of European Fascism,* Universitetsforlaget: Oslo, pp. 26–51.

Hahn, C. L. (1996) Research on issues-centered social studies, in R. W. Evans and D. W. Saxe (eds.) *Handbook on teaching social issues,* Washington D.C.: National Council for the Social Studies, pp. 25–41.

Hahn, C. L. (1998) *Becoming political: Comparative perspectives on citizenship education,* Albany: State University of New York Press.

Hahn, C. L. (1999a) *Educating a changing population: Challenges for schools,* Halle Institute Occasional Paper, Atlanta, GA: Emory University.

Hahn, C. L. (1999b) Challenges to civic education in the United States, in J. Torney-Purta, J. Schwille and J. A. Amadeo (eds.) *Civic education across countries: Twenty-four national case studies from the IEA civic education project,* pp. 583–607. Amsterdam: The International Association for the Evaluation of Educational Achievement.

Hahn, C. L. (2002) Preparing 21st century citizens, *Monograph for Scott Foresman social studies series,* Chicago: Scott Foresman.

Halman, L. (2001) The European Values Study: A Third Wave, *Source Book of the 1999/2000 European Values Study Surveys*, Tilburg University.

Harber, C. (1994) International Political Development and Democratic Teacher Education, *Educational Review*, 46, 2, 1, pp. 59–65.

Haste, H. and Torney-Purta, J. V. (1992) *The development of political understanding: A new perspective,* San Francisco: Jossey-Bass.

Havel, V. (1990) New Year's Address to the Nation, in *Congressional Record-Extension of Remarks,* vol. 136, no. 2, January 24, 1990, 149.

Heater, D. (1974) History Teaching and Political Education, *London Politics Association*, Occasional Pamphlet, no 1.

Heater, D. (1978) History and Political Literacy, in B. Crick and A. Porter (eds.) *Political Education and Political Literacy*, London: Longman.

Heater, D. (1983) The origins of CEWC (Council for Education in World Citizenship), paper presented at a *seminar in the Department of Educational Studies*, University of York.

Heater, D. (1990) *Citizenship: The civic ideal in world history, politics and education*, London: Longman.

Heater, D. (1999) *Citizenship: what is it?* Cambridge: Polity Press.

Hepburn, M. (2000) Service learning and civic education in the schools: What does recent research tell us? in S. Mann and J. Patrick, *Education for civic engagement in democracy: Service learning and other promising practices,* Bloomington, IN: ERIC Clearinghouse for Social Studies/Social Science Education. pp. 45–59.

Hirschman, A. (1977) *The Passions and the Interests,* Princeton: Princeton University Press.

Hirschman, A. (1982) *Shifting Involvements. Private Interest and Public Action,* Princeton: Princeton University Press.

*History and the Core Curriculum 12–16. A Feasibility Study for Comparative Research in Europe* [Report of a CIDREE Workshop, Madrid, November 1992] (Dundee, June 1993).

Hladnik, M. (1995) All Different – All Equal: who defines education for citizenship in a new Europe? in A. Osler, H-F. Rathenow and H. Starkey (eds.) *Teaching for Citizenship in Education.* Stoke on Trent: Trentham.

Holden, C. (1999) Education for Citizenship: the contribution of social, moral and cultural education, in A. Ross (ed) *Young Citizens in Europe.* London: CiCe.

Horton, J. (1984) Political Philosophy and Politics, in A. Leftwich (ed) *What is Politics?* Oxford: Blackwell.

Hunt, M. P. and Metcalf, L. E. (1968) *Teaching high school social studies* (2nd edition), New York: Harper and Bros.

Inglehart, R. (1977) *The Silent Revolution,* Princeton: Princeton University Press.

Inglehart, R. (1990) *Culture Shift in Advanced Industrial Societies,* Princeton: Princeton University Press.

Inglehart, R. (1997) *Modernization and Postmodernization. Cultural, Economic and Political Change in 43 Societies,* Princeton: Princeton University Press.

Irish National Teachers' Organisation *(1999) The Challenge of Diversity.* INTO Publications: Dublin.

Jackson, J. (1999) Historians and the nation in contemporary France, in S. Berger, M. Donovan, K. Passmore (eds.) *Writing National Histories,* London and New York: Routledge, 205–16 and 239–51 respectively.

Kastoryano, R. (2001) Nationalité et citoyenneté en Allemagne aujourd'hui, *Vingtième Siècle. Revue d'histoire,* avril–juin 2001, no. 70, pp. 3–17.

Kerr, D. (2000) Citizenship Education: an international comparison, in D. Lawton, J. Cairns and R. Gardner (eds.) *Education for Citizenship,* London: Continuum.

King, R (1979) *All things bright and beautiful? A sociological study of infant classrooms.* Chichester: Wiley.

Köln, Germany: Zentralarchiv für Empirische Sozialforschung/Ann Arbor, MI: Inter-university Consortium for Political and Social Research [distributors] 1999.

Lahlou, S. (1998) *Penser Manger,* Paris: Presses Universitaires de France.

Lang, Jack and Lean-Luc Mélenchon (2001) *For a European 'desire to live together'*, part of the Programme of the French Presidency of the European Union, Division of Education (2001).

Lapierre, J. W. (2001) *Qu'est-ce qu'être citoyen?* Paris: Presses Universitaires de France.

Lasch C. (1979) *The Culture of Narcissism*, New York: Warner Books.

Ledeen, M. A. (1979) Renzo De Felice and the Controversy over Italian Fascism, in G. L. Mosse (ed), *International Fascism: New Thoughts and New Approaches,* London and Beverly Hills: Sage, pp. 125–41.

Lee, P. and Ashby, R. (2000) Learning History, in P.N. Stearns, P. Seixas and S. Wineburg (eds.) *Knowing Teaching and Learning History*, London: New York University.

Lee, P. Dickinson, A. and Ashby, R. (1994) There were no facts in those days: Children's Ideas about Historical Explanation, in M. Hughes (ed) *Teaching and Learning in Changing Times*, Oxford: Blackwell.

Lipovetsky, G. (1983) *L'ère du vide*, Paris: Gallimard.

Lister, I. (1991) Research on social studies and citizenship education in England, in J. P. Shaver (ed), *Handbook of research on social studies teaching and learning.* New York: Macmillan, pp. 602–609.

Lochak, D. (1991) La citoyenneté, un concept juridique flou, in D. Colas, C. Emeri and J. Zylberberg (eds.) *Citoyenneté et nationalité. Perspectives en France et au Québec*, Paris: Presses Universitaires de France.

Margerison, C. (1968) Island: A social studies experiment, *Ideas, 8/9,* Goldsmith College Curricuklum Laboratoory.

Margerison, C. (1972) A learning experiment in social studies education: aspects of children's political understanding and development, *Teaching Politics*, 1, 2, pp. 14–18.

Mazower, M. (1999) *Dark Continent. Europe's Twentieth Century,* Harmondsworth: Penguin, Ch. 7.

Méchet Ph. and Weill P. (2000) L'opinion à la recherche des citoyens, Ch. 9, in B. Badie and P. Perrineau (eds.) *Le citoyen. Mélanges offerts à Alain Lancelot*, Paris: Presses de Sciences Po.

Meier, K. and Kirchler, E. (1998) Social representations of the euro in Austria, *Journal of Economic Psychology*, 19, 6, pp. 755–774.

Melich, A. (1999) Eurobarometer 47.2OVR: *Young Europeans*, April–June 1997 [computer file], Brussels, Belgium: INRA (Europe) [producer].

Milward, A. S. (1997) The springs of integration, in P. Gowan and P. Anderson (eds.) *The Question of Europe*, London: Verso.

Montané, M. (1995) *The Regions and Europe: The European Dimension in Secondary Education: Study Materials for Teacher Education,* Barcelona: Collegi Oficial de Doctors i Llicentiats en Filosofia i Lletres i en Ciencies de Catalunya.

Morabito M., Bourmaud, D. (1993) *Histoire constitutionnelle et politique de la France (1789–1958),* Paris: Montchrestien.

Morton, T. (no date) *Co-operative Learning and Social Studies: towards excellence and equity,* Kagan Co-operative Learning.

Moscovici, S. (1961) (edition of 1976) *La psychanalyse, son image et son public*, Paris: Presses Universitaires de France.

Moscovici, S. (1989) Des représentations collectives aux représentations sociales, in D. Jodelet (ed) *Les représentations sociales*, Paris: Presses Universitaires de France, pp. 62–66.

Mossuz-Lavau, J. (1994) La politique Janus, Ch. 7, in P. Perrineau (ed) *L'engagement politique*, Paris: Presses de la Fondation nationale des sciences politiques.

Müller-Peters, A. *et al.* (1998) Explaining attitudes towards the euro: Design of a cross-national study, *Journal of Economic Psychology*. 19, 6, pp. 653–680.

National Council for Curriculum and Assessment (NCCA) *(1996)*, *Civic, Social and Political Education*, *Dublin: NCCA.*

Newman, M. (2001) Allegiance, Legitimation, Democracy and the European Union, HEC 2001/5, Florence: EUI Working Papers.

Newmann, F. and Wehlage, G. G. (1993) Five Standards of Authentic Instruction. *Educational Leadership*, 53, pp. 8–12.

Niemi, R. and Junn, J. (1998) *Civic education: What makes students learn,* New Haven: Yale University Press.

Niemi, R. and Smith, J. (2001) Enrolments in high school government classes: Are we short changing both citizenship and political science training? *PS: Political Science and Politics, 34*, 281–288.

O'Donoghue, J. (2000) Speech of the Minister for Justice, Equality and Law Reform, John O'Donoghue at the launch of the *Irish Government, Interdepartmental Working Group Report* on the Integration of Refugees in Ireland in 2000. Irish Times, 10 February 2000.

Orwell, G. (1945) *Animal Farm*, London: Secker and Warburg (edition of 1951: Penguin).

Osler, H. (1994) Education for Development: Redefining citizenship in a pluralist society, in A. Osler (ed), *Development Education: Global perspectives in the curriculum,* London: Cassell.

Parker, W. C. (1996) *Educating the democratic mind,* Albany, N.Y.: State University of New York Press.

Parker, W. C. (2001) Toward enlightened political engagement, in W.B. Stanley (ed), *Critical issues in social studies research for the 21st century,* Greenwich, CT: Information Age Publishing, pp. 97–118.

Paxton, R. O. (2001) *Vichy France: old guard and new order 1940–1944,* New York: Columbia University Press.

Pepermans, R. and Verleye, G. (1998) A unified Europe? How euro-attitudes relate to psychological differences between countries, *Journal of Economic Psychology*, 19, 6, pp. 681–700.

Perrineau P. (1996) L'engagement politique: déclin ou mutation? *Futuribles*, Oct. 1996, no. 213, pp. 5–16.

Pike, G. and Selby, D. (1988) *Global Teacher, Global Learner,* London: Hodder and Stoughton.

Pinkel, F. (2000) *The European home: representations of 20th century Europe in history textbooks,* Germany: Council of Europe Publishing.

Pring, R. (1999) Political Education: relevance of the humanities, *Oxford Review of Education,* 25, 1 and 2, pp. 71–88.

Qualifications and Curriculum Authority (QCA) (1999) *Consultation on the Secretary of State's proposals for a revised national curriculum in England* Circular 27/99, London: QCA.

Qualifications and Curriculum Authority and Department for Education and Employment (QCA/DfEE) (1998) *Education for Citizenship and the Teaching of Democracy in Schools.* London: QCA/DfEE.

Qualifications and Curriculum Authority and Department for Education and Employment (QCA/DfEE) (2000) *Citizenship in the National Curriculum.* London: QCA/DfEE.

Report on the Implementation of the Resolution of the Council and the Ministers of Education meeting within the Council of 24 May 1988 on the *European Dimension in Education,* Brussels: Commission of the European Communities, 1993.

Resolution of the Council and the Ministers of Education meeting within the Council of 24 May 1988 on the European Dimension in Education, *Official Journal of the European Communities,* no. C177, 6–7–88, Luxembourg: Office for Official Publications of the European Communities, 1988.

Riches, J. (1974) Education for Democracy: A curriculum unit for Upper Juniors, *Teaching Politics,* 3, 2, pp. 121–126, and second part *Teaching Politics,* 3, 3, pp. 199–206.

Robins, L. and Robins, V. (1978) Politics in the First Year: this year, next year, sometime, never, *Teaching Politics,* 7, 2, pp. 137–147.

Roland-Lévy, C. (1998) Economic socialization, in P.E. Earl and S. Kemp (eds.) *The Elgar Companion to Consumer Research and Economic Psychology,* Cheltenham and Nortampton, Ma: Edward Elgar, pp. 174–181.

Roland-Lévy, C. (2000a) Developing identities via different social representations. Teenagers, unemployment and ideology, in A. Ross (ed) *Developing Identities in Europe,* London: CiCe.

Roland-Lévy, C. (2002b) Economic Socialisation: How does one develop an understanding of the economic world? in M. Hutchings, M. Fulop and A-M. van Den Dries (eds.) *Young People's Understanding of Economic Issues in Europe,* European Issues in Children's Identity and Citizenship 2, Stoke on Trent: Trentham Books, pp. 17–30.

Roland-Lévy, C. (2002c) Passage du Franc à l'Euro: Représentation sociale et attitude, *Les Cahiers Internationaux de Psychologie Sociale,* 55, 2002 (forthcoming).

Rosanvallon, P. (1992) *Le sacre du citoyen,* Paris: Gallimard.

Ross, A. (1981) Using literature to develop political concepts in the primary school, *Teaching Politics,* 10, 1, pp. 85–96.

Ross, A. (1999) What concepts of identity lie behind 'European Citizenship'? in A. Ross (ed) *Young Citizens in Europe*, London: CiCe.

Schoulz, J., Säljö, R. and Wyndhamn, J. (1997) Heavenly talk. Discourse, artifacts, and children'sunderstanding of elementary astronomy. Paper presenterat vid 7th European Conference for Research on Learning and Instruction (EARLI) i Aten, August 1997.

Scottish Consultative Council on the Curriculum (1996) *Sharing responsibility: ideas for integrating a key aspect of the European dimension into the curriculum,* Dundee: SCCC.

Seixas, P. (2000) Schweigen! Die kinder! Or, does Postmodern History Have a Place in the Schools? in P. N. Stearns, P. Seixas and S. Wineburg (eds.) *Knowing Teaching and Learning History*, New York and London: New York University.

Selbourne, D. (1994) *The Principle of Duty*, London: Sinclair Stevenson.

Sennett, R. (1974) *The Fall of Public Man*, New York: Alfred A. Knopf, Inc.

Shore, C. (2000) *Building Europe: The Cultural Politics of European Integration,* London: Routledge.

Short, G. (1999) Children's grasp of controversial issues, in M. Woodhead, D. Faulkner and K. Littleton (eds.) *Making Sense of Social Development*, London: Routledge.

Slater, J. and Hennessey, R. (1978) Political Competence, in B. Crick and A. Porter (eds.) *Political Education and Political Literacy*, London: Longman.

*Social and Community Planning Research*, British Social Attitudes Survey, 1998 [computer file]. Colchester, Essex: The Data Archive [distributor], 8 June 2000. SN: 4131.

Soysal, Y. (1994*) Limits of Citizenship*, Chicago: Chicago University Press.

Sternhell, Z. (1986) *Neither Right nor Left. Fascist Ideology in France,* Berkeley and Los Angeles: University of California Press.

Stevens, O. (1979) Politics and the Juniors: The political thinking of younger children, *Teaching Politics*, 8. 3, pp. 263–272.

Stevens, O. (1982) *Children Talking Politics: Political Learning in Childhood*, Oxford: Martin Robertson.

Stradling, R. (2001) A Council of Europe Handbook on Yeaching 20th Century European History, in J van der Leeuw-Roord (ed) *History for Today and Tomorrow: What does Europe mean for School History? (pp 230–248).* Hamburg; Korber-Stiftung.

Stradling, R. (2001) *Teaching 20th Century European History.* Strasbourg: Council of Europe Publishing.

Talbot, M. (1999) Can values be taught? in *The Tablet*. October 9, pp. 1353–54.

Titchiner, B. (2001) Democracy in action – a student led workshop demonstrating the workings of the democratic meetings at Summerhill School in A. Ross (ed) *Learning for a Democratic Europe*. London, CiCe. pp 123–126.

Topf, R. (1995) Electoral participation, in H.D. Klingemann and D. Fuchs (eds.) *Citizens and the State*, Oxford: Oxford University Press.

Torney, J., Oppenheim, A. and Farnen, R. (1975) *Civic education in ten countries,* New York: John Wiley. ED 132 059.

Torney-Purta, J., Lehmann, R., Oswald, H. and Shulz, W. (2001) *Citizenship and education in twenty eight countries; Civic knowledge and engagement at age fourteen,* Amsterdam: The International Association for the Evaluation of Educational Achievement. www.wam.umd.edu/~iea/

Torney-Purta, J., Schwille, J. and Amadeo, J.A. (eds.) (1999) *Civic education across countries: Twenty-four national case studies from the IEA civic education project,* Amsterdam: The International Association for the Evaluation of Educational Achievement.

UNESCO/CIDREE (1983) *A Sense of Belonging: Guidelines for values for the humanistic and international dimension of education.*

van Everdingen, Y. M. and van Raaij, W. F. (1998) The Dutch people and the euro: A structural equations analysis relating national identity and economic expectations to attitudes towards the euro, *Journal of Economic Psychology,* 19, 6, pp. 721–740.

van Kersbergen, K. (2000) Political allegiance and European integration, *European Journal of Political Research,* 37, pp. 1–17.

Vaus, de D. (2002) *Surveys in Social Research,* London: Routledge.

Vergès, P. (1985) Une possible méthodologie pour l'approche des représentations économiques, *Communication Information,* VI, 2–3, pp. 375–396.

Vergès, P. (1992) L'évocation de l'argent: une méthode pour la définition du noyau central d'une représentation, *Bulletin de Psychologie,* Special Issue: *Nouvelles voies en psychologie sociale,* XLV, no. 405, pp. 203–209.

Vergès, P. (1998) Représentations sociales en psychologie économique, in C. Roland-Lévy and P. Adair (eds.) *Psychologie Économique. Théories et Applications,* Paris: Economica, pp. 19–33.

Vergès, P. and Bastounis, M. (2001) Towards the investigation of Social Representations of the Economy: Research methods and techniques, in C. Roland-Lévy, E. Kirchler, E. Penz and C. Gray (eds.) *Everyday Representations of the Economy,* Austria: WUV Universitätsverlag, pp. 19–49.

Wade, R. C. (1997) *Community service learning: A guide to including service in the public school curriculum,* Albany, NY: State University of New York Press.

Wagstaff, S. (1978) *Teacher's Guide: People Around Us – 1: Families,* London: Inner London Education Authority.

Wolfs, R. (1992) *Geography and History with a European Dimension. Manual for teachers in secondary education,* Enschede: Hans Hooghoff, Marita Tholey.

189

# Index

Active citizenship/participation 37, 42–45
asylum seekers 117–8

CiCe vii, 23
citizenship 2, 13, 22–25, 48, 94, 112–2, 126–7, 133–5, 137–46, 165
citizenship education 12, 20–22, 41–6, 78, 124, 129–20
concepts 10, 18, 25–6, 27, 30, 37
concepts, procedural 10–11, 38, 39–43
Continuous Tracking Survey 13, 94

Davies, I. 7, 10, 34–52, 177
democracy 24, 79, 84, 163–4
Denmark 30–2, 45, 84–6

Edye, D. 4, 7, 13, 94–115, 177
England 17–33, 34–52, 83, 88, 109–12
ethnocentrism 64–7
euro/eurozone, EMU 15, 146–51
Eurobarometer 13, 98–100, 101–109, 132
Europe 1, 6–7, 95
European citizenship 13, 20–21, 51–4, 96–8, 102–5, 112–4, 153
European Values Survey 14, 15, 129, 132, 138, 149, 161–75

Feertchak, H. 3, 7, 14, 126–146, 177
France 57–9, 66, 75, 109–12, 127–30, 147–60

Germany 57–8, 66, 82, 86, 89, 134

Greece 60, 67

Hahn, C. 9, 12–13, 78–93, 177
history (school subject) 11–12, 48–50, 53–77
human rights 96, 98, 112–25

identities, multiple 4, 96
identies, nested 22
identity 1, 3, 167–8, 144–5, 110–1
Ireland 116–125

Kallis, A. 6, 11–12, 53–77, 177
Kekhofs, J. 3, 15–16, 161–176, 177
Killeavy, M. 7, 14, 116–125, 178

language (school subject) 49

migration, refugees 14, 117–8

nation states 5
nationalism 54
Netherlands 78, 83, 88

participation, civic 42, 91–3, 128–9, 142–3, 166, 173
personal and social education 34, 48–50
political alienation 7–8, 13, 23–4, 135–6, 163
political education 3, 8, 17–20
political identity 2, 137–46
political issues in learning 28–9, 30–3
political literacy 34, 36

191

political understanding/socialisation 25–6, 137–8
politicians 23–25, 43, 90
politics 36–37

racism 102–2, 118–20
refugees 116–25
Roland–Levy, C. 1–16, 147–160, 178
Ross, A. 1–16, 17–33, 178

schools and schooling 9
service learning 12–13, 43, 173

single-issue politics 24–25, 43, 91, 128, 164–5
Spain 109–11

teachers, role of 30–32
territoriality 129–30, 148, 155–6
textbooks 73–6
Thorpe, T. 7, 10, 34–52, 178
tolerance 101–2, 162–3, 167

UK 1–16, 17–33
USA 82, 87

# European Issues in Children's Identity and Citizenship 3

# POLITICAL LEARNING AND CITIZENSHIP in Europe

Edited by Christine Roland-Lévy and Alistair Ross

This series offers a timely observation of the changes in young people's socialisation in Europe. How young people learn to understand their own societies and the societies of their neighbours will influence the future development of social and political institutions. The ways higher education institutions educate social workers, teachers, early childhood workers and youth workers about social understanding and learning needs to be informed by contemporary European policies and practices.

This series comments on current developments and research. Published in association with CiCe – the European Union Thematic Network Programme 'Children's Identity and Citizenship in Europe' – the volumes offer reflection, analysis and contextualisation of recent findings, locate these in pedagogic practice, and point to their educational implications.

This volume examines children's and young people's conceptualisation of political institutions and concepts. Political understanding empowers individuals to cope with the demands and opportunities afforded by citizenship. We need to learn more about how children and young people understand personal, national and international political phenomena, and consider how schools can further their understanding. What do they understand about power, justice, rights and responsibilities? This volume surveys the different age groups in Europe for whom personal, local, national and international contexts are significant.

Contributors: Ian Davies(UK), Dave Edye (UK), Helene Feertchack (France), Carole Hahn (USA), Aristotle Kallis (Greece), Jan Kerkhofs (Belgium), Maureen Killeavy, (Ireland), David Leiser (Israel), Zsuzsa Matrai (Hungary).

**ISBN I 85856 276 7**

**Trentham Books**

www.trentham-books.co.uk

Children's
Identity &
Citizenship
in Europe

562766

781858

9